FROM CUBS TO SPITFIRES

MY LOVE AFFAIR WITH AVIATION

Rudy Frasca

Dedicated to:

This book is dedicated to many people I have known over the years. First and foremost, to Lucille, my soul mate and partner. To all the pilots I have met and flown with over the years and to all those we have lost in flying accidents. To my children and grandchildren and with great dedication to my son Joe who was an inspiration to all who knew him and saw him fly. And to all who are involved with any aspect of aviation. Let's keep this great industry thriving!

CONTENTS

CONTENTS

INTRODUCTION

My father Rudy is an amazing man. Unlike many people, he found his passion early in life and was able to make it his livelihood. And like so many successful men of his era, he was not a stellar student, did not have financial backing and made his way in the world with what he refers to as "moxie". His dream was to start a flight simulator business, sell maybe 50 simulators and have twelve kids! Although he and my mother stopped at eight children (which I'm sure was okay with her), his business went on to deliver well over 2000 flight simulators worldwide and is still going strong.

In the early days of Frasca Aviation (the company's original name), my father traveled a lot and my mother raised us without a nanny, housekeeper or disposable diapers (a feat any mother can appreciate). She cooked, cleaned, even sewed us clothing, and kept eight kids (five boys, three girls) under semi-control while dad was out drumming up business and designing flight simulators. I have many fond memories of him returning from exotic locales with souvenirs for us kids. I'm sure my mom had many fond memories of him returning - period! There is a saying that behind every successful man is a strong woman and my dad acknowledges this every day, saying things like, "that Lucille is a real winner" or "I'm so lucky to have your mom, I don't know why she puts up with me."

As the company grew, so did my dad's airplane collection. He loved all types; gliders, his favorite Piper Cub, Cessna 152, 172, and 182, our beloved Mooney, Beech Bonanza, Turbo Commander, etc.., And of course….. The Warbirds. We kids grew up thinking going to the airport to look at planes and go flying was a natural weekend event. I have many memories of flying out to breakfast with dad and whoever else showed up on the weekend for the flight to "Arnies" or wherever they decided to go. Once I even flew with him in the back of the T-34 when he decided to do aerobatics without telling me first. Not a fun experience!

Dad's first warbird was an FM2 Wildcat. After that, he added (in no particular order) a P-40, SNJ, T-6, Fiat, two Spitfires, FW190 and many others. Eventually, he purchased an airport and in 1990, he built a new factory to house Frasca International next to the airport (aptly named "Frasca Field"). Since then, the company has steadily grown, going through some ups and downs, but coming out stronger due to my dad's continued passion and belief that his simulators help to train better and safer pilots.

Although my dad's hobbies were pretty limited to flying and anything aviation, he has always been a family man and was a great role model for a husband and father. His dream was to have all of his children learn to fly and eventually join him in his business. While not all of us are active pilots, most of us did learn to fly and all of us at times have been involved in the family business.

My parents are extremely strong people. They were raised during the depression and have great discipline and fortitude. When my oldest brother, Joe, died in a plane crash in 1991, they were naturally devastated, however, they showed such strength and faith that I would forever be in awe of them. Joe was a talented aerobatic pilot and the oldest son. We all looked up to him. After my brother's funeral, we had a large gathering at our airport; it was a celebration of Joe's life. A missing man formation was performed and as anyone who has experienced that can attest, it is moving beyond words. That was my father's gift to us. He taught us how to celebrate life in the face of loss.

Anyone who knows Rudy knows that he is bigger than life and a natural story teller. Over the years, he started writing down anecdotes about his flying adventures and really, anything having to do with airplanes. It seems like he has been working on "his book" forever and so when he asked me to help him put it together for printing, it seemed like it was long overdue. So, here are his stories in no particular order. They are aviation tales yet they parallel many life experiences and stages. Pilots and non pilots will get a kick out of "Rudy's adventures." Enjoy!

—Peggy Frasca Prichard

A Brief Biography:

Born in Melrose Park, Illinois on April 19, 1931, the fourth child of Italian immigrants, Rudy Frasca began taking flying lessons at the age of 14 and soloed shortly thereafter. In 1949, Rudy joined the Navy and was stationed at Glenview Naval Air Station, where he worked as an instructor teaching pilots on the early Link trainers. After the Korean War, he left the Navy to attend the University of Illinois, where he did research in Aviation Psychology and honed his interest in the field of flight simulation.

In 1958, Rudy put together everything he had learned in the Navy and the University, and built his first flight simulator at home in his garage; and Frasca Aviation was founded (the name later changed to Frasca International to reflect the emerging character of the business). Today, the name "Frasca" is often used as a generic term for simulators and has become a household word in the aviation training community. Although the company has grown dramatically, Rudy's original mission remains the same: to design and manufacture high quality flight simulators for training pilots worldwide.

With over 65 years of active flying, Rudy is active in many areas of aviation and has held every office in the Warbirds of America organization. He has been a member of the Experimental Aircraft Association (EAA) since 1956 and is a founding member of the Sport Aviation

Association. In the year 2000, he was appointed to the Governor's Board of Aeronautical Advisors. He was previously a member of the NATA Flight Training Committee and is currently a member of the University Aviation Association (UAA) and the Council on Aviation Accreditation (CAA).

Rudy has received numerous awards both for his personal efforts and Frasca International's success in the simulation industry. Among these awards for his contributions to the field of aviation is the "Lifetime Patron and Fellow" award from the University Aviation Association. He has been inducted into the Chanute Air Force Base Hall of Fame for lifetime support to Chanute Air Force Base in Rantoul, Illinois. He has been recognized by the Warbirds of America for his outstanding contributions to the Warbird movement and excellence in Air Show Flying, and was named to the Illinois Aviation Honor Roll in 1993 for outstanding contribution to the promotion and advancement of aviation in the state of Illinois. In 1994, Rudy was awarded the W.W. Estridge, Jr. Award by the University Aviation Association "in recognition of a lifetime of dedicated service to general aviation education". He was also presented with the Charles Lindberg award for "Outstanding Contribution – Industry", at the 1994 National Magnet School Convention for "outstanding corporate support, magnet school partnerships, continuous and generous outreach and superb national leadership in and for the magnet schools of America". In 1996, he received the Governors award for "Continuing Export Excellence" in the state of Illinois. Also, in 1989 he was awarded the Illinois High Tech Entrepreneur award and was named the "top small business" in Champaign County.

In 2000, Rudy Frasca was chosen by the Illinois Department of Transportation's Division of Aeronautics to represent the state of Illinois in the National Aviation Hall of Fame Exhibit and Learning Center located at the US Air Force Museum at Wright Patterson Air Force Base, Dayton, Ohio. In 2002, he was presented with the University Aviation Association's President's Award for his lifelong commitment to the UAA and the collegiate aviation community. Only two of these awards have been given in the organization's 55-year history.

In May 2012 Rudy was inducted into the NAFI (National Association of Flight Instructors) Hall of Fame.

In the Beginning:

CHAPTER 1

The Day Dad and I Finally Understood One Another

Whether flying is your career or your hobby, you don't forget the people you have met along the way. Unless you're wealthy, learning to fly almost always means making financial sacrifices; you automatically have two things in common with many others: You love flying and you're usually broke! I remember how I lived day-to-day, earning enough money for my next flight.

When I was in high school I worked at my uncle's nightclub washing dishes, peeling potatoes, cleaning up and doing anything else he wanted. I would work from 6 p.m. Friday night until 3 a.m. Saturday morning for five dollars to earn enough money to take flying lessons. I would go home after work, sleep for three hours, then get up early morning and walk three and a half miles to the airport for a flying lesson. My dad was always very supportive of this often grueling schedule, except once; the PT-19.

I got it in my mind that I was going to get checked out in the PT-19, a WWII trainer with a 160 horsepower inverted Ranger engine. To say it was an exciting experience after flying the Piper Cub would be an understatement. The catch was that the airplane rented for $19 an hour. When you consider it was a macho aircraft, and the price also included the instructor, it really wasn't such a bad deal. But $19 was still a lot of money in those days.

I had been pretty enthusiastic about the whole idea and certainly didn't hide my intentions, but dad didn't catch wind of what I was up to until the day I had enough money to do it. I was half way along my three-and-a-half mile trek to the airport when dad's car abruptly pulled up alongside me in a cloud of dust. He opened the door and, in a controlled but firm voice, said in his Italian accent "Get in."

I could always tell when my father was upset because his Italian accent got just a tad bit thicker as he reigned in his temper. "You are not going to spend $20 on flying" he said, "that's too much money!" But I was determined to get checked out in the PT-19 and decided to appeal to his reason; I knew if I became argumentative I would lose the battle very quickly. "Pa," I said, "I work long hours at the club to earn money for flying lessons. You agreed that whatever I earned I could spend on flying." As I looked into his eyes staring back at me I could see the mixed emotions. On the one hand $19 was a lot of money and to him flying represented little more than a hobby. He found it very difficult to conceive of the idea of spending that much money on something like flying. On the other hand, he knew I worked very hard to earn that money. As he sat there looking at me, contemplating how I could have worked so hard and still be willing to spend so much, I think for the first time he realized that flying was more than my hobby; it had become the core of who I was. Dad put the car back in gear and drove me to the airport. He dropped me off in silence but it wasn't that icy silence of a battle lost, rather it was one in which he struggled to understand how important this really was to me. To the best of my recollection, from that day forward, my dad allowed me to chart my flying career in whatever manner I deemed appropriate. But his wisdom regarding the $19 checkout didn't escape me either. Almost immediately after getting checked out in the PT-19 I came to the realization that I simply couldn't afford to fly it with any regularity. In the end, I was financially forced to move back to the J-3 Cub at a more affordable $6 an hour. And, without any further discussion on the subject, my dad and I each learned something from one another. He learned that I too had dreams worth pursuing at any cost, and I learned that a very real part of following one's dream is to assess the cost verses benefit.

CHAPTER 2

Meeting Lucille

It was in July 1954 that I found myself driving to the south side of Chicago and parking in front of 8240 South Sangamon for a blind date with Lucille Matern. I recall vividly a rather robust gentleman standing in front of the apartment building watering the lawn; his resemblance to the Union Leader John L. Lewis was a bit disconcerting. I walked up to him and respectfully said "Good morning, sir" causing him to carefully look me up and down. It turned out he was the owner of the tri-level apartment building, so I asked him which apartment was Lucille's. In ritualistic male fashion, we stood momentarily sizing each other up. Eventually, he finally made a "harrumph" sound, apparently not impressed by my very dark tan and my old white naval pants and t-shirt, and told me which apartment.

The encounter with "John L. Lewis," who turned out to be Lucille's father, along with the idea of a blind date, combined to make me somewhat nervous. So it was with some trepidation that I knocked on the apartment door. The door opened and there stood this gorgeous-looking gal with dimples and a ponytail! Suddenly, any doubt I had vanished from my mind and it was full speed ahead! She showed me in and introduced me to her mother, who, it turned out, was a great cook. As I ate a hearty breakfast and drank coffee I met her father, brother and sisters. The plan for the day included my taking Lucille to

Elgin Airport, west of Chicago, for some glider flying. Lucille packed a bag full of food for the outing which could have fed us like kings for a week in Alaska; I was really beginning to like her family.

We had a great time on that first date and continued to see each other regularly. Of course, I was still commuting back and forth between Chicago and Melrose Park every weekend. With Lucille now a prominent and ever-growing part of my life, I also was making numerous trips on weekends to the south side of Chicago to pick her up. And because we went flying gliders, we'd often go all the way out to Elgin from her house. By the end of 1954 I was astounded to discover I had put 33,000 miles on my car that year! I like to joke about how I decided to propose to her because I figured it would be cheaper to marry her and move her down to Champaign with me. The truth is, when we were together it would always be in the back of my mind that in a day or two we'd be apart for a week or more. When I was in Champaign I kept thinking about Lucille and missing her. I was hooked and there were no two ways about it.

We got married and I had two goals in those days: I wanted to own my own simulation factory and, being a good Catholic, I wanted 12 kids. Lucille, who never actually objected to 12 kids, would get a somewhat strange smile on her face when I would talk about the idea. We set up housekeeping in the Champaign-Urbana area so I could continue school, and I also continued working in the University's Aviation Psychology Department. A few years later, we started our own simulation company in addition to my work at the university.

Lucille and I nurtured our family and our fledgling business, watching them both expand and get stronger. After the birth of our eighth child, Lucille's smile got perceptibly tighter when I'd talk about the goal of 12 kids. Somehow, by the kind of unspoken agreement that all married couples can produce, the business continued to expand and the family stopped at eight kids. None-the-less, I was as happy as could be. I still had a large family, with no future prospect of having to change diapers again – the idea of grand parenting had yet to occur to me – and I finally had my own simulation factory together with Lucille.

Ever since the first time Lucille opened that apartment door in 1954, I have considered myself one of the luckiest men in the world. I have led my dream life with her helping me every step of the way. I hear of other people who have problems in their marriages, and I can't imagine what that would be like; ours has been so ideal. Of course, I do kind of wonder what this chapter would say if Lucille were writing the book. At this writing, Lucille and I have been married 56 years. In addition to our 8 children, we have 18 grandchildren.

CHAPTER 3

My First Luscombe

Back in 1949 there were four of us that flew together fairly regularly. Our interests were alike at that time, so we decided to enter into a partnership and purchase an aircraft together. One of us got to talking one day with Ed Prosperi who owned his own airport in Tinley Park, south of Chicago. He said he had a nice '41 Luscombe for sale, and we all made the trip to Prosperi Airport to take a look at her. After some hemming and hawing, the four of us struck a deal with Ed to buy the Luscombe for $650. She was worth every penny of it.

We emptied out our pockets and among us we had a total of $50 which we gave Ed as a deposit, shook hands on it, and went home with plans to return the next day and pick her up. On the way home the sky began getting dark and ominous, but we didn't think much about it. That night a terrific thunderstorm swept over the south side of Chicago and seemed to focus its fury on Prosperi Airport. When we arrived back the next day, there was the Luscombe, totally destroyed. Ed felt really bad about the whole thing and shaking his head he gave us back our $50.

During the ride back home, we lamented the loss. We had all pretty much gotten used to the idea of having our own airplane in one night and were now faced with the reality of being airplane-less once again. So, we just kept looking around and talking to folks until we turned up another Luscombe. This one was a 1946 Model 8A with a 65 horsepower engine that was in even better condition. Again we hemmed and hawed with the owner and ended up also buying that one for $650.

Our group held together fairly well for about two years, getting plenty of use out of the 8A. Eventually other priorities began diverting everyone's attention away from the Luscombe. So when the opportunity arose, I bought out my partners. I was in the Naval Reserves full time by then and based at Glenview Naval Air Station, north of Chicago. Even though I had bought a used car for about $100 and the airplane, my $24 a week from odd jobs and my monthly Navy pay still went pretty far because I had practically no other expenses. I can remember thinking back then that I spent more per week on gas for the airplane and car than anything else; aviation fuel was $0.25 per gallon then. It helped that the people I took flying paid for the gas.

For the next few years, that Luscombe and I became very good friends, and long after I sold it I would think back on those happy days together. Years later, I would find an almost exact duplicate of that airplane and buy it purely out of nostalgia. The Luscombe is now stored number one in our museum hangar. Over the years, I flew it more than any of my other airplanes.

CHAPTER 4

How I Lost My First Luscombe

To say I was broke when I first attended the University of Illinois would be an understatement. All I had to my name was a Luscombe worth $600 and two suitcases full of clothes. I could fly home to visit my parents, who lived west of Chicago in the quaint Italian suburb of Melrose Park, but because I didn't have a car, I had no way to get back and forth between campus and the airport! Sometimes a good friend of mine, Jack Lambie, would loan me his bike; but from time to time, I would have to figure out another means of transportation to the airport. So, I'd find out who owned a car, and when I needed to go to the airport, I'd offer to give them an airplane ride. One way or the other, I always made it out to the airport.

I really enjoyed that Luscombe and flew it as often as I had the time and the money for gas. I flew her about 350 hours, much of which was aerobatics. One of my favorite pastimes was to get a lot of altitude then shut off the engine and ease the nose up until the prop stopped. Then I'd glide dead stick as long as possible, enjoying the quiet and scenery. It was the closest thing I could imagine to being a bird. Eventually I'd tuck the nose down to build up enough airspeed to get the prop to turn again and restart the engine; it didn't have such luxury equipment as a starter. Well, it was just a lot of fun, and I'll admit after a while I got a bit over-confident and careless in the aircraft.

So, it was on December 22, 1952 I planned to take off from the University Of Illinois Airport to fly to Woodale Airport, west of Chicago, to visit my parents for Christmas. After getting a ride to the airport, I realized I didn't have enough money for gas and borrowed it from the lady at the airport snack bar. Eventually I got the Luscombe in the air and turned north toward Chicago. Just past Kankakee, 85 miles north, the weather began to deteriorate rapidly with the ceiling and visibility getting very low. As the ceiling forced me closer and closer to the ground, I realized that the visibility was so bad that the cars were moving very slowly. I decided I'd better find a place to land as soon as possible and started looking for a suitable field.

Within a minute or two, the visibility was low enough that I had to put her down in a field right alongside the road I was following. I observed there were some very high wires on the approach end, but it otherwise appeared to be a good choice. I turned left from north to west, cleared the wires, and went into a steep slip until just before touch down. The field, it turned out, was very soft and the wheels quickly dug in causing the aircraft to flip tail over nose onto its back. After everything got quiet, I hung there upside-down for a few seconds and then, without thinking, I made the mistake of unbuckling my seatbelt. After rearranging myself from the obvious effect of gravity, I opened the door and crawled out of the aircraft. Looking over the airplane, I realized that she did not just simply flip over and stop instantly in the dirt. It had slid upside-down for some distance, rudder first, causing the fuselage to crinkle.

I hated to leave the Luscombe lying there in the mud, she looked so sad, but there was nothing else I could do. I hitchhiked to my parents' house and explained the situation to them. My mother almost fainted! We talked about how to get the aircraft out of the field and decided the best course of action would be to find a suitable trailer and haul her out. Fortunately, I was a member of the Chicagoland Glider Club, and Joe Trefny, one of the members, had a glider trailer which he agreed to loan to me. The next day we drove down to the field, took off the wings, loaded her on the trailer, and brought her back to the University Airport.

In retrospect, I should have rebuilt the Luscombe. She was a great little airplane, and years later I would buy another one, out of nostalgia, that was almost identical. But at the time, I really didn't know any better, so I decided to sell her for parts. That left me without an airplane and without much money, so I made a deal on a 1946 Aeronca Champ. While the Champ wasn't that old, it had about 11 coats of dope which made it unusually heavy. The first thing I did was add a cruise prop to get the greatest possible airspeed for the 130 mile trip from Champaign to Chicago but the Champ had a tired engine. So, I switched it with the Luscombe engine, which was a bit better, and on a good day, she would cruise at 85 mph. Still, the excess weight combined with the cruise prop really had a negative effect on her takeoff performance. It wasn't too long before someone bought the landing gear off the Luscombe, and then she looked pretty sad. Soon after, Professor Oliver Luerssen from Normal, Illinois expressed an interest in buying what remained. Talk about negotiations! By the time we had an agreement, I had $192.50, a motor scooter, and two popcorn machines. It was a good deal for me because I ended up with spending money, ground transportation and a source of income. I put the popcorn machines into two fraternity houses on the University of Illinois campus where they began earning me money! Between sons John, Tom, and myself, we later had three Luscombes in the family at one time which were all eventually sold.

CHAPTER 5

An Expensive Wedding Ring

Over the years, I've considered myself a very fortunate man when it comes to my wife Lucille; she's one in a million. I remember my nephew, Chris Matern, telling me a few years ago about his fiancée who insisted that he give her a diamond engagement ring equal in value to his most expensive toy. Unfortunately, his most expensive toy was his $50,000 airplane. He thought long and hard on the subject and finally came up with the only reasonable solution: he kept the airplane and found a more understanding fiancée.

In 1954, when Lucille and I got engaged, she wasn't so demanding; but then again, times were different. Unfortunately, though, I found myself short of money when it came time to buy an engagement ring. So, one afternoon I took my 1943 Taylorcraft up for one last flight then sold her for $250 (which happened to be the price of the engagement ring I bought for Lucille at an auction). Things were simpler in those days, and sacrifice was the norm, not the exception. She loved the ring, and though I felt sad at losing the T-Craft, I soon discovered there were more and different airplanes to buy and fly as our financial condition permitted. As good an airplane as it was, I've never regretted trading that T-Craft for the engagement ring.

UPDATE: The diamond was found to be a fake! When Lucille later went to get the ring remounted, she was told that the stone was cracked, which obviously meant that it wasn't a diamond. It appeared that Lucille was looking at my Spitfire. When in a romantic mood, I asked Lucille if I should buy her another but more valuable ring. She replied that she was not materialistic, and the current ring had a special meaning. (Remember that $250 was all I had.)

After we got married, I gave her two coupon books. These were for monthly payments toward our car and on our air conditioner. Although I was a student at the University of Illinois, I did have a job. She also got a job with the University, so we made the payments. After a year or so, the babies started coming, and she stopped working outside the home. That's another story!

CHAPTER 6

Flying the Old-Fashioned Way

When Lucille and I first moved to Champaign in 1955, after we were married, we moved into an efficiency apartment owned by the University of Illinois. The little one-room apartment had a small cubicle for a kitchen and a very small bathroom. We qualified for the apartment because I was both a student at the university and employed by the University of Illinois.

While the days were filled with classes and work, I still had this growing need to restore another airplane; a task that was not going to be made any easier without a garage to work in. Lucille and I talked it over and she agreed that I should start looking for a suitable, meaning inexpensive, airplane, and rent a garage. The speed with which I found a 1946 Taylorcraft BC12D fuselage to buy and a two-car garage to rent amazed her; I was back in the flying business.

Shortly after taking over the garage I located a 75-horsepower Continental engine and put it next to the fuselage; they were quickly joined by a propeller. As I watched parts accumulate I began to notice a lack of wings. So I put out the word I was in the market for suitable wings. Almost immediately they seemed to find their way into the garage. At one point I counted seven T-craft left wings! By then I had hired a couple of part-time mechanics, and together we were able to disassemble one of the wings, reverse it, and manufacture a right wing. The rebuilding of the individual pieces to make each airworthy continued at a steady pace, however, there was a dark cloud looming on the horizon. I didn't have the paperwork required by the FAA to make this emerging airplane legal in their eyes.

Fortunately, a Taylorcraft dealer named Charlie Harris had the paperwork and name plate that belonged to a wrecked airplane; it was exactly what I needed. By that point we had gotten the various components assembled, but there just wasn't enough room in the garage to attach the wings and all the components on the fuselage; so we moved everything down to the hangar of a good friend named Skeezicks in Tuscola, IL, 25 miles south of Champaign. Despite his rather colorful image, one that got more colorful with the passing years, Skeziks knew just about all there was to know about antique and classic aircraft. His advice and guidance, as well as his hangar space, were invaluable.

My excitement grew everyday as I watched the T-craft get closer and closer to completion. Finally, the magic day arrived and I found myself behind the controls of the newly rebuilt airplane. I was of the opinion that she would be a very spunky aircraft which was to be proven very quickly.

It is normal after totally rebuilding an airplane to do some low- and high-speed taxi tests before actually attempting to fly the airplane. The idea is to get a feel for it, make sure everything pretty much works the way you think it should, and, to a somewhat lesser degree, that all the parts will hold together. I did a few low-speed taxi tests then moved on to the high-speed tests when the T-craft got tired of such foolishness and just popped off the ground and started to fly. I quickly landed it.

As I expected, the Taylorcraft had really good performance. So much so, in fact, that I decided to put a tow-hook on it so that I could tow gliders. And, while the airplane had adequate power for towing, it was still relatively lightweight. One summer afternoon I was towing gliders and the lift was so good that after I got up to altitude and released the glider, I dove down and dropped the tow rope, returned to the same thermal I had found with so much lift, shut off of the engine and climbed 1000 feet in the thermal as if I were flying a glider too!

The T-craft was beginning to remind me of another old friend. I used to go up to about 5,000 feet in my old Luscombe, kill the ignition, slow the airplane down until the propeller stopped turning, then fly it around "dead stick" for awhile, taking advantage of thermals to slow my rate of descent. After awhile, I'd turn the ignition on, dive the airplane to build up speed, and eventually the airspeed would force the propeller to start turning again. Once the prop began to turn the fuel would flow, the mags would create spark, and the engine would restart. Dumb? Sure, I guess so, but it was also lots of fun. And, if the engine didn't restart, which occasionally it wouldn't, well, that's why we always made sure we played the game in the vicinity of an airport so we could just land dead stick. Today, that would be called an emergency.

I remember doing that one day near Glenview Naval Air Station, before I went into the Navy and was stationed there. The engine wouldn't restart so I was forced to dead stick it on the military installation. Here was this little Luscombe landing between two Corsairs on the southwest runway. Immediately after touching down and rolling off to one side, a Naval Chief appeared at the airplane and he wasn't happy. I casually said "carburetor icing" and he just looked at me hard, walked up front and hand-propped me to get the engine started. I waved, taxied away and took off. Try that today and you'll end up with a full-scale, joint FAA and DOD investigation.

I guess a devil-may-care attitude was somewhat prevalent in those days. There was the time I was flying with Bill Hrebick in a 1946 Piper PA-12. The airplane had a 100 h.p. engine with tandem seating. The PA-12 was very modern as it had a starter and ignition key so you didn't have to prop the airplane to get it started. Bill was flying from the front seat and I was sitting in back watching the scenery slide by. As we passed over the old Douglas Airport, which eventually became

O'Hare International, Bill switched off the ignition, pulled out the key and threw it over his shoulder onto my lap. He then proceeded to fly around a while as we slowly descended and until he made a dead stick landing on the airport. The airport had very little traffic then. Just about every time I fly into O'Hare I think about that incident and wonder what Air Traffic Control would say if I tried to do that today on exactly the same spot.

The whole idea of dead stick landings was to be totally proficient in the event of an engine failure. Playing those sorts of games was not just dare-devil; it did have a purpose, though I suspect there was a bit of devil in instructors when they'd do it to their students. Back in the days before Champaign Airport had a tower, we often had our students dead stick land at the conclusion of a lesson. I recall that with a new student, to get him used to the idea of dead stick landings, I had a little ritual I used. Back in those days, instructing for the university, we used to fly the Aeronca 7AC Champion, a 65 h.p. training aircraft that did not have the luxury of a starter. If you stopped the prop in the Champ near the ground it was just about impossible to get her restarted in the air.

After a new student had completed the lesson, I would take over the controls while still at a fairly high altitude but in the vicinity of the airport. Much to the student's dismay, I would shut down the engine, proceed to do some dead-stick aerobatics followed by an approach to the airport. I would then land dead stick by first touching down on one wheel, then the other wheel, and finally taxi back with just the remaining momentum of the airplane. Most students really thought that was great fun but a few kissed the ground when they got out of the airplane. Times were sure different back then.

CHAPTER 7

How I Ended Up
Buying an Airport

One question that I am often asked is how I came to own an airport. People seem to expect there is some exotic story associated with it, but the truth is actually pretty simple and straight-forward.

Frasca Field, originally called Illini Airport, is located in the northeast corner of Urbana, Illinois. It has been continuously operated as an airport since 1940. Prior to that time, the ground was originally farm land owned by the Dyson family whose son Louie had more than a passing interest in the art of flying. In that year, his passion for flying exceeded his farming interests, and Illini Airport was inaugurated.

Illini Airport immediately became a popular local airport with a steadily growing business until World War II when everything slowed down. When the war ended and the G.I.'s returned home, they had flight training veteran's benefits burning a hole in their pockets. Very quickly, Illini Airport became a hub for ex-G.I.s who wanted to learn how to fly. Its reputation firmly established, the airport continued to attract flight students training under the G.I. Bill after the Korean and Vietnam Wars as well as students without veteran's benefits. It also earned the respect of countless local business and private pilots as well as transient pilots.

By the late 1970's, Louie Dyson was quickly approaching the age of 65. He'd gotten to that point in his life where Central Illinois winters were no longer beautiful and fascinating; he was spending most of the winter in Florida. It was pretty clear to everyone that Louie was more than contemplating retirement. But unlike most businesses, it's not so easy to sell an airport. He thought about the people he knew, and my name flashed through his mind. I was in the aircraft simulator business, travelled regularly in my own aircraft on business. I owned several of my own aircraft, which I had based at the University Of Illinois Willard Airport. So, he approached me about buying his airport. I'll admit I thought about it for a day or so, the idea having some appeal to be sure; but in the end, I decided I had too much going on to even consider owning an airport. So I called Louie the next morning and gracefully told him I wasn't in a position to consider it at that time.

By the summer of 1980, Louie Dyson still hadn't sold his airport, and I had pretty much forgotten about the whole idea. Then one beautiful summer day, I decided to take my Cessna 170 for a ride. It was still based at Willard Airport along with my Wildcat, P-40, and Mooney. After an otherwise uneventful but enjoyable flight, I was returning to Willard Airport and dutifully contacted Approach Control. I was asked to squawk ident on my transponder for radar confirmation; the only problem was I didn't have a transponder. Knowing full well that I was not required to have a transponder I confidently replied, "Negative on the transponder", to which he just as confidently replied "leave the Airport Traffic Area, and I'll contact you in about 10 minutes, we're too busy right now!"

As I flew around killing time outside the Airport Traffic Area, I was at first a bit angry, but that quickly gave way to a much more deep seated concern. I suddenly began to realize how many small airports that I had known as a kid in Chicago were either no longer in existence or had grown, gotten control towers, and were becoming more and more inhospitable to good, old fashioned, grass-roots, general aviation. Refocusing on Willard Airport I recalled the days, only a few years before, when you could easily come and go without a radio let alone a transponder. Well, before the Approach Controller called me back, I'd made up my mind. I was not going to let Illini Airport get shut down; I would buy it! I then picked up the microphone, changed frequencies from Willard Approach Control to Willard Tower and, ignoring Approach Control altogether, I asked Tower for permission to land. "Cleared to land runway 22" was their immediate response, as if confirming there was always plenty of room for a soon-to-be airport owner at their airport.

I had so much conviction in my voice when I talked to Lucille about it that she didn't once question my sanity. The final terms were 20% down with a 10 year note. Need I mention we had to borrow the 20% down payment? And so, on July 8, 1980, Lucille and I became the proud owners of Frasca Field, destined to become the world head-quarters of Frasca International, Lucille's Hot Dog Stand and Flying School, and a museum. But that's another story. Years later when I related this story to John and Martha King, owners of the well-known King Schools, John quipped, "It would have been cheaper to buy the transponder."

I must add that this experience with the tower operator is not a negative commentary. The tower and its operators are first class and do go out of their way to handle aircraft operations in a friendly and professional manner. I made a bigger thing out of this case to justify buying the airport – and in the end it worked!

The Warbirds
(and other airplanes)

CHAPTER 8

My First Warbird

During the 1950's and 60's I owned a number of aircraft for various reasons, but you couldn't really say I was "collecting" airplanes. For most of my life, however, I have been thrilled by the sight of World War II fighters. Called "warbirds" by those who collect and admire them, the old aircraft are not only historic but are very exciting to fly. Rarely does a warbird owner simply fly the aircraft. Most owners also fly aerobatics, perform at air shows, and display their aircraft at air shows all over the country during the summer. It's safe to say that for most owners warbirds are more than a hobby, they are a way of life.

In 1968, while working a booth for our simulators at the helicopter convention in Anaheim, California, my interest in warbirds became more focused. It was there that I ran into Frank Tallman and Frank Pine from Tallmantz Museum; these two guys lived, slept and ate warbirds! So I got to chatting with Tallman about the pros and cons of different warbirds. The more we talked, the more I wanted to have one for myself. After a while I finally asked him which warbird he'd recommend for me. He thought for a second and said, "Well, since it's not likely you'll be flying into combat in the near future, I think either the P-40 or the Wildcat would give you a good start and let you sort of grow into it." He went on to explain that each aircraft would be a challenge to learn to fly really well but neither would be too difficult in which to get started safely. After that conversation I knew I wanted a Wildcat for a number of reasons.

The Grumman Wildcat was the first successful American shipboard fighter and is considered to have contributed most to the tilting of power in the Pacific during WWII. It was the first U.S. aircraft in British service to shoot down a German machine in WWII when, on December 25, 1940, two Wildcats (then called Martlets) intercepted and destroyed a Junker JU 88.

A lend lease version of the Wildcat (flown from the British carrier Illustrious) participated in the landings on Madagascar and allied invasion of North Africa during which a Martlet, which was the British version of the Wildcat, operating from the British carrier Victorious took surrender of the French fighter base at Blida.

By 1942, the U.S. equipped all its carrier fighter squadrons with the Wildcat, and it remained the sole American shipboard fighter for the first part of the war. It participated in all major naval battles and destroyed 905 enemy aircraft during 1941-43 for the loss of 178 machines.

The first Wildcats to fight in the Pacific were of VMF-211 serving on Wake Island. The epic defense of the island by VMF-211 was to become legendary. In the first Japanese attack on the island on December 8, 1941, eight of the twelve Wildcats were destroyed, but the remaining four were flown continuously, fighting heroically for two weeks, breaking up many air attacks, and sinking a cruiser and a submarine with 100 pound bombs before the last two Wildcats were destroyed on December 22, the day the Japanese landed on the island. During the next few months, Wildcats took part in a series of raids against Japanese held islands, and they provided fighter cover for the U.S.S. Hornet during the famous Doolittle raid on Tokyo. It is during this period of time LTC John S. Thach perfected his noted maneuver, the weave, and LT Edward H. (Butch) O'Hare gained fame when, on February 22, he destroyed five Japanese twin-engine bombers while alone defending his carrier. O'Hare International Airport in Chicago was dedicated to him.

In May and June of 1942, the two decisive carrier battles of Coral Sea and Midway were fought, and Wildcats managed through excellent pilot training, efficient combat formation and Japanese tactical errors, to overcome the high performing Zeros and contributed significantly to the American victories. These are the battles that stopped the forward thrust of the Japanese. Later that year and in early 1943, the Guadalcanal based Wildcats of Marine squadrons achieved spectacular success in reversing the Japanese thrust. Among the noted pilots taking part in the these operations was CPT Joseph Foss who, on January 15, 1943, became the first WW II U.S. pilot to equal Eddie Rickenbacker's score of 26 kills in WW I.

In February, 1943, Vought F4U-1 Corsairs began to replace Wildcats in land-bound operations squadrons, and in August 1943 the Grumman F6F-3 Hellcats made their combat debut. Since the smaller and lighter Wildcat was ideally suited to the shorter decks of escort carriers, it continued service in convoy escort and ground support of amphibious forces. Wildcats played a significant part in the capture of the German submarine U-505 now on display at Chicago's Museum of Science and Industry.

Well, my mind was made up, I would buy a Wildcat; and it seems once you decide you're going to buy one, word gets out pretty quickly. It wasn't long before someone gave me Jack's name.

Jack had a Wildcat FM-2 for sale that was based at Westchester County Airport in Pennsylvania. More important, Al Sheves, a good friend of mine, had been doing all its maintenance. I called him and said I was thinking of buying the Wildcat, and he verified it was in good condition and would be a good deal. I called Jack, and we talked about the airplane quite a bit. It was obvious he really liked it and had some strong feelings. He talked about how good it was, how well it flew, and its excellent condition. We finally got around to the topic of price and hammered out $15,000. I was definitely sold and quickly mailed a deposit check for $7,500.

About a week later, I flew commercial airlines there and brought a check for the balance. When flying the Wildcat, like most warbirds, the pilot should wear a parachute, so I carried one with me on the airline. I don't know if it was my imagination or not, but it seemed no one wanted to sit near me on that flight! Anyway, I was certainly looking forward to completing the transaction for the Wildcat and flying it home. But, in the intervening week, Jack got to thinking about the Wildcat. Perhaps it was our telephone conversation that mustered up too much nostalgia for the old airplane, but the deal didn't work out. Jack decided he just didn't want to part with it, and there was nothing left for me to do than to return home. I was disappointed, but I could understand how he felt.

Despite my disappointment, my interest in buying a Wildcat grew stronger. I began reading "Trade-A-Plane," a periodical that has extensive listings of aircraft for sale, and before long I found one for sale in Atlanta. It turns out, I had seen this Wildcat at air shows and knew first-hand it was really special. It had been meticulously restored by Dick Lambert and Mike Retke, two Delta Airline pilots, and was in great shape. I called them right away and, without any fanfare, but with a bit of haggling, we finally agreed on $28,500. This time I gave them no chance to change their minds and promptly got them to commit.

Dick put two externally mounted wing fuel tanks on the aircraft to give it an additional 120 gallons for the trip to Champaign. Since it was a single seat aircraft, and I had never flown a Wildcat, Dick agreed to fly it to Champaign for me. It turned out that the wing tanks slowed the airplane down about 20 knots, but the aircraft proved to have more fuel than necessary because, when he landed in Champaign, the main tank had never been used. We removed the wing tanks from the aircraft, and they now hang from the rafters in the Frasca Air Museum to this day.

Once in Champaign, I gave Dick a check for $28,500. Dick then gave me a thorough cockpit checkout, and talked to me about handling and performance characteristics. He then talked me through an engine run-up, and supervised me while I did a little bit of taxiing around the airport. After a while I taxied back to the ramp and shut it down. Dick then shook my hand, offered me his congratulations on becoming an honest to goodness warbird owner, and then caught the next flight back to Atlanta. Suddenly, it occurred to me that I owned a big, powerful, World War II fighter I had never actually flown before.

For several days, I just taxied that aircraft around the airport: low speed taxi, high speed taxi, you name it. I called a friend that had an AT-6 "Texan," which was a two seat trainer that had been used to get pilots ready to transition to the Wildcat during the war. After some dual with him in the AT-6 I taxied the Wildcat some more. In all, over the next few days, I must have spent about four hours taxiing all over the airport, trying to get a feel for the Wildcat and build up the nerve to fly it. I was getting so good at taxiing that one afternoon on the inactive runway, which, because of a wind change became active; the tower controller quickly came over my headset and asked "What are your intentions?" Well, I felt ready, so I answered, "I'll be taking off and heading west".

I applied takeoff power and was immediately impressed by the increased performance over anything else I had flown. But what surprised me the most was the tremendous increase in the cockpit noise with the engine at takeoff power. Other than that, it became very clear why the "Texan" was used as a dual trainer: there were no surprises, and the takeoff went very smoothly.

The heading took me over a Boy Scout camp that my son, Joe, was attending. I circled it a couple of times. Joe mentioned later that the campers were all excited and waved when Joe said it was his dad.

After some air work, I returned back to the airport for my first approach and landing. I was concentrating so hard on doing everything perfectly that it actually all came out well. I was surprised how well the aircraft landed, and I continue to be surprised that the old saying is true. Your first takeoff and landing are often the best you'll ever do!

I must confess that the future landings in the Wildcat were more difficult than many other aircraft that I flew. The landing gear is not that wide causing the Wildcat to tilt in cross winds. The Wildcat was designed for carrier landings and takeoffs when the wind would be from directly ahead.

CHAPTER 9

The Wildcat

When my FM-2 Wildcat was originally restored in about 1965, it was outfitted with a Wright 1820-87 engine. The -87, rated at 1200 hp, was used by the Army Air Corps to power the B-17, the Lockheed Lodestar, and a few other aircraft; it was never used by the Navy. The Wildcat, a Navy airplane, actually used the 1350 hp, 1820-56 version of the engine. As it happened, the people who overhauled what would become my Wildcat had more time than money and used an available -87 taken off of an old Lodestar. With approximately 700 hour's total time, the engine ran satisfactorily and they made the decision to not overhaul it.

One of the concerns common to most round engines is the oil tends to flow into, and fill, the lower cylinders when it is not running. This causes a potential hydraulic lock problem when you try to start the engine. As the pistons on those lower cylinders try to move into the cylinder on startup they are held back by the oil which is unable to go anywhere else. The starter generates enough power that it can cause the piston rod to bend as the piston is not allowed to move forward because of the hydraulic lock. Consequently, one does not just hop into that type of aircraft and hit the starter. Standard procedure is to pull the propeller through by hand until at least 7 propeller blades pass by. At that point, the pistons will have moved through all the cylinders and you are assured that there is no hydraulic lock. It is then okay to start the engine.

It, on the other hand, you are pulling the blades and encounter strong resistance, you probably have a hydraulic lock. In that case, you must remove the spark plugs from the bottom cylinders to allow the oil to drain out through the spark plug holes. Once the oil is drained, it is a good idea to start the engine and let it run with the bottom cylinder plugs removed. A dirty job, to say the least, it is the only way to be sure that the engine in cleared of all excess oil. At that point, you would clean and reinstall the plugs, then go through the normal engine start procedure. Obviously, operating round engines can be somewhat of a burden but we had ten aircraft in our collection that used them, so we'd become fairly accustomed to their unique requirements.

Our particular engine had a real tendency to leak oil when it was sitting in the hangar. There was an oil shut-off valve that blocked the flow from the oil reservoir tank to the engine. It was standard procedure to turn off that valve after shutting down the engine if the airplane wasn't going to be used for an extended period of time. Of course, it was critical to turn it back on before starting the engine.

Not long after I bought the Wildcat I had it at Oshkosh. Some friends and I were planning on flying North of Oshkosh for a ride in our airplanes so I did a quick engine run up to warm it up and check it out before the agreed departure time. The airplane was still fairly new to me and I liked to make sure everything was alright in advance of a planned flight. Once I was satisfied, I shut down the engine and waited for my friends to show up.

Before long we were all assembled, started up our aircraft, taxied out and took off to the North. Soon my engine began to heat up and the oil pressure began to drop. It was pure chance that I happened to look at the instruments just as the problem began but I knew I would have to act fairly quickly. Glancing to my right, I recognized Appleton Airport and immediately turned directly toward a runway. Just as I touched down the engine froze up and the propeller quit turning. The thing that was hard for me to understand at the time was that the oil valve was turned on, but in recollection I realized what I had done. I had run up the engine the first time without turning on the oil valve. The oil in the lines had been mostly used up during that earlier run-up so that there was a line full of air waiting to work its way to the engine during my second start.

We towed the aircraft over to the KC Aviation's hangar on the airport where some very good friends of mine worked. We tested the engine and found a tremendous amount of metal in the oil; it was beyond rebuilding and never ran again. They agreed to replace the engine for me. I knew there would be some increase in performance as a result of going from 1200 to 1350 hp but I was surprised by how much. It hadn't occurred to me that my old engine wasn't simply a 1200 hp engine but a very tired 1200 hp engine. On the way back to Champaign, after I picked up the Wildcat with a newly overhauled engine, I just kept smiling.

CHAPTER 10

And Then
There Were Two...

I had been flying my Wildcat for some time and enjoying it, but I began to notice the P-40 more and more. I thought it looked very sleek and kept recalling that Frank Tallman had said it, too, would be a good warbird to own. The more I thought about it and saw others, the more I realized that I would inevitably end up with a P-40. The history of the P-40E that I finally did purchase is typical of the strange history of that model aircraft.

It was built in 1940 and slated for shipment to England on a lend-lease program. Somehow the aircraft got sidetracked to Canada and remained there for the duration of World War II. After the war, the entire group of P-40E's of which it was a part, were sold as surplus. Oddly enough, many of them, including mine, were purchased by farmers for as little as $50! These weren't Flying Farmers either. They were interested in the fuel, wheels, and tires to be used for their tractors. One farmer buried a P-40 in his backyard. It was dug out and sold years later and rebuilt to flying condition.

My particular P-40E was purchased by a farmer for $50 and apparently, rather than stripping it down for parts, he later sold it to someone else for $600. The airplane sat for some years until a pilot named Bill Ross bought it for $12,000 and brought it to DuPage Airport, just west of Chicago. Bill kept it in his hangar, and Dip Davis, a mechanic that worked on Bill's fighter collection, set out to restore it.

Bill held on to the aircraft for some time and never quite got around to finishing it. He got wind of my interest and offered the aircraft to me for $26,000. I was ready to buy it and went so far as to build a long garage behind my house big enough to restore it. Bill and I talked it over, and I wasn't sure if I was willing to buy it outright for the asking price or whether he and I would just build it up together.

While Bill and I were having these discussions, Don Plumb, one of our Warbird members and a friend from Windsor, Canada, heard Bill had it and called to express his interest. Bill told him he was already negotiating with me, so Don called and asked how interested I was in the airplane. I thought it over and felt that Don was "in the family" so to speak, and the P-40E would really be "home" in Canada. After some thinking I agreed to let Don have it, although I claimed first right of refusal should he change his mind or desire to sell it later. Don bought the aircraft and quickly started restoration, but before the airplane was completed he was killed in a P-51 accident. Once again the P-40E was available.

Somehow along the way, Bill Ross and another warbird friend, Max Hoffman, laid claim to having the first right of refusal. After everyone talked it over, Max bought the aircraft and did an absolutely beautiful job of its restoration. He did such a good job that it rightfully took 1976 Grand Champion at the annual Oshkosh fly-in. He flew it for a while and then offered the aircraft for sale once again. Remembering my history of "always a bridesmaid, never a bride" when it came to purchasing the aircraft, he called me first to ask if I was still interested. By then, I had put it out of my mind and told him that one Warbird per person was enough! Max laughed and said, "Rudy, you've been bitten by the warbird bug and you only live once!"

Well, I started thinking about what Max had said. He was right; I was bitten by "the bug." So I began analyzing the whole project. After putting pencil to paper, I called Max back and told him I thought it really did make sense. He immediately suggested $130,000, which I thought was a fair price considering it also included some spare parts. The next thing I knew Max flew the P-40E to Champaign from Fort Collins. It was not only a beautiful airplane but excellent to fly as well; it had clearly deserved to win Grand Champion.

In September, 1979, pictures of our P-40 and Wildcat were used to illustrate an article in The National Geographic magazine. Shortly afterwards the editor forwarded a letter to me from Mrs. Jane Petach Hanks. It read as follows:

"The Flying Tiger decorated P-40 that appeared in your September issue 1979, jumped out at me because it bore the number 47. That was the number of my husband's plane that I anxiously awaited to return many times in China in 1942. He was John Petach, Squadron leader of the Second Squadron, the Panda Bear, of the American Volunteer Group or the Flying Tigers.

The plane that Rudy Frasca flies is decorated exactly as John's plane, except the Panda Bear should have a mustache, wear boots, and be riding a bicycle. Each member of the Second Squadron had a Panda Bear painted on the fuselage of his plane with the characteristics of its pilot. John, or "Pete" as he was called, had a dark mustache, wore "cowboy" boots, and rode a bicycle.

I was a nurse for the Flying Tigers. "Pete" was killed flying on a bombing and strafing mission ten days after the Flying Tigers were officially disbanded. I returned home that year with his child. "In the movie "Flying Tigers", John Wayne courted a nurse. John Wayne played the part of "Tex Hill". Tex later told me that he did court her.

CHAPTER 11

Platinum Plugs and the P-40

I received a telephone call one day from the folks at Flying Magazine. I was told they were developing a special issue on warbirds, and they wanted to know if I would fly my P-40 to the upcoming Reading Airshow in Pennsylvania where it would photographed. They wanted to use it for some special ads they were going to run that included a very well-known personality. I told them I'd be happy to help out, and we made the necessary arrangements. Unfortunately, there was one, small problem with the airplane that I would have to consider.

A few weeks prior, I had been flying the P-40; and during an approach to Purdue Airport in West Lafayette, Indiana there was suddenly a strong smell of fuel. When I looked down on the floor of the cockpit, I noticed a growing puddle of avgas forming around my feet. Considering I was just about to flare for landing, I decided there wasn't much more I could do but land and shut it down as quickly as possible. Being prudent, however, I decided to not retract the flaps after landing because the electric pump motor was located next to the fuel cell behind the cockpit. The landing was uneventful, and I taxied briefly and shut her down. In retrospect, I should have shut it down and gotten out quickly as soon as it stopped, even on the runway!

After a thorough inspection, I found that the rear tank was badly leaking. The tank was original equipment, installed during World War

II, and had simply deteriorated over the years to the point where it had now begun to leak. Since the front two tanks were still in good condition, I decided to empty the rear tank, close it off to the rest of the system, and operate on the two remaining good tanks. While that was acceptable from a safety point-of-view, it only left a total fuel capacity of 87 gallons resulting in an operational problem which would cause me to make more frequent fuel stops.

So, with a limited fuel capacity, I commenced my flight from Champaign, Illinois to Reading with a planned fuel stop at The University of Ohio airport in Columbus. The trip there was uneventful; but as they were refueling the aircraft, Jack Eggspuehler came walking across the ramp. He took one look at my P-40 and teasingly said, "You sure know how to hurt a guy, don't you?" It was obvious he liked the P-40, and coming from him that's a real compliment. Jack owned a P-51 Mustang for a while.

Jack's a pillar in the general aviation community and was instrumental in the formation of the National Association of Flight Instructors. I'd known Jack since the days when we both worked at the University of Illinois. Over the years, we had many occasions to work together on various projects such as the AOPA 180 and 360 programs. Jack and I chatted for some time until I remembered that I still had at least another hour of flying ahead of me to get to Reading. So I did a preflight, said goodbye to my old friend, climbed back into the P-40, and continued on my way.

Perhaps I'd lingered a bit too long in Ohio talking with Jack. The forecast for scattered clouds ended up turning into broken and, before long, overcast. As a precaution, I leaned the fuel back considerably and continued the flight. When I finally arrived north of Reading, I was VFR-on-top of a solid overcast. I contacted approach control and asked for a clearance and radar vectors to the airport. They asked me to squawk ident on the transponder but were unable to receive my signal, so I was cleared into a holding pattern. While in the hold,

I began to calculate my original 87 gallons of fuel against about an hour of flight time up to that point.

Normally, the aircraft would burn about 60 gallons an hour, and even though I had leaned it out considerably during cruise, I decided I'd better lean it out as much as possible now that I was stuck in the hold. I began pulling the power back slowly, as far as I could, and ended up at about 1650 RPM. Then I reduced the manifold pressure to about 15 inches; she really slowed down. I was just holding altitude but really conserving on fuel. I had never been able to lean the aircraft out that low before. Finally, after about a half hour in the hold, I was given approach vectors to the airport. I broke out under the overcast and landed. When I shut down the engine on the ramp I recorded one hour and forty-five minutes total time. After having the aircraft refueled I discovered that it only took 46 gallons; I was astounded!

The photo session went very well, and we were pleased to see the P-40 when it appeared in Flying Magazine. When I returned home from the trip, I talked to our mechanic and related the incident to him. We agreed that the better fuel consumption could be attributed to the fine wire, platinum plugs we had recently installed. Prior to that, we had always used the more conventional, massive plugs. It turned out that the platinum plugs permitted a much lower power setting, but how much lower ended up being a very pleasant and cost-effective surprise!

CHAPTER 12

Flying Tigers

I wasn't old enough to serve during WWII, let alone be a pilot in the famous American Volunteer Group (AVG), also known as the Flying Tigers, but I received a letter including an invitation to their 50th anniversary reunion. It was to be held on July 4, 1991 in San Diego, CA. and I quickly accepted it.

A good friend, Paul Poberezny, was to receive special recognition from the group during this event. Paul is probably best known for founding the Experimental Aircraft Association but is very active in many facets of aviation including warbirds. I couldn't help but wonder where, in a house whose walls are already covered with so many awards and plaques, he would put yet another, but I did want to be on hand for the ceremony.

Another reason for attending was to visit with our many good friends who really had been pilots and crewmen for the AVG. Long ago we painted our P-40E in the distinctive AVG colors which featured the famous "Flying Tiger" teeth on the nose of the aircraft. Our P-40E, with its faithfully reproduced tiger, serves as a magnet at the various air shows we attend. If there's an ex-AVG member at the Airshow, he'll very likely end up standing by our airplane in short order. This has led to many friendships with personnel who really served in the AVG. And to a man, I have always admired those brave men and two women nurses who voluntarily went to defend China before the U.S. entered into the war. They gave up their personal safety, comforts of home, their businesses, and families. They were true heroes.

So it was that Lucille and I attended the 50th Anniversary Reunion. We participated in meetings, dinners and hospitality suites and had opportunities to join the "Flying Tigers" over an extended period of time. Although the members of this elite group were all, at this time, in their late 70's and early 80's, it appeared that no one had bothered to tell them they had gotten older. While I wasn't around at the time they were "active," it is difficult for me to imagine they could have been more animated or heartier. It certainly doesn't appear that they've changed much from those early days. To put it mildly, they really enjoyed raising a lot of hell. (Lucille and I attended hospitalities each evening, usually leaving them at about midnight.) We were invariably the first to leave as the Tigers waved goodnight and continued drinking, laughing and reminiscing. The first morning, after some late night hospitality parties, Lucille and I awoke fairly early to go to breakfast. When we got to the restaurant there were very few people besides us. I commented to the waitress how we went to bed early and as a result could get up earlier than the older guys. She laughed and said they'd long since finished breakfast and were all back in the hospitality suites going full strength. It was a ritual that would continue throughout the reunion!

One of the primary reasons for attending the reunion was to be present for an historic occasion. Although the Flying Tigers played a very important part in fighting the Japanese in China and Burma, they were never formally recognized by the United States government. They were, after all, civilians who chose to go to China to fight without any official attachment to the U.S. Armed Forces. It was at this 50th Anniversary Reunion that the United States Congress officially recognized the men of the American Volunteer Group for their contribution. As a result, surviving AVG members are now eligible for veteran's benefits.

A fitting, but long-overdue, honor to those who truly volunteered to make the world a safer place in which to live.

Madame Chiang Kai-shek sent each member of the Flying Tigers a large signed picture of herself standing with her husband General Chiang Kai-shek and General Claire Chennault. This was in 1991, and she was still alive to sign them.

The picture I now have was given to me by John Young.

General Chiang Kai-Shek with his wife and General Claire Chennault

CHAPTER 13

The Real Story behind the Bent Props

Over the years, a lot of people have commented about three bent propellers that I have on display. They came from my FM-2 Wildcat. The story goes all the way back to 1972.

In those days, a friend by the name of Don Plumb used to put together an annual Airshow at his home-base airport in Windsor, Ontario, Canada. Don invited 50 to 60 warbirds to participate. The warbirds would provide aerial entertainment including aerobatics, fly-bys and dogfights. Don also made sure there were lots of static displays. With Detroit just across the river, there was always a good-sized crowd. It was a great combination of old friends, lots of fans, and great parties. Don's Airshow was one of the more enjoyable ones in which we participated.

During the Airshow, I found myself in a fly-by routine of about 50 warbirds. During one fly-by, I made what's known as a "dirty pass" straight down the runway about 50 feet high. A "dirty pass" means my landing gear was fully extended, and the flaps were down. Normally, that is the configuration used for landing; but in this instance I didn't actually expect to be cleared to land. Instead, I was making a dirty pass for effect. At that slow a speed, the other warbirds just zipped right by me at 250-300 mph. It looks really nice from the ground. It was fantastic from my vantage point!

I fully intended to "clean up" the airplane's configuration (raise the gear and flaps) and go-around to rejoin the line and wait my turn to land. So, I was surprised to hear the tower clear me to land ahead of everyone else upon completion of my low pass! Well, I can tell you the prospect of landing first rather than lining up with 50 other airplanes was most inviting. I maneuvered around to a very short approach to the runway. To this day I can remember a voice in my head telling me to go around just as I was about 10 feet off the runway and flaring the airplane to land. Something didn't feel right, but in that instant I just shrugged my shoulders and continued the approach.

The gear collapsed on touchdown. It could have been avoided by going-around and recycling the gear. I can tell you one thing for sure; the Wildcat doesn't slide on its belly very far down an asphalt runway. I do remember looking out the window during the slide; at that point I was just a passenger seeing the prop stop when it hit the ground. When the airplane finally came to rest, I quickly released my seat belt and parachute, jumped out, and ran away from it just in case it caught fire. Overhead, 49 warbirds were circling because I was blocking the only runway. I remember a friend of mine, Ormond Haydon Bailley, made a low pass in his Sea Fury to see if I was okay, and he saluted me as he went by. He was wearing a WWII helmet, and it felt as if I were suddenly transported back in time - as though I had been shot down.

I stood there, a few yards away from my FM-2 Wildcat, worth $50,000 at the time, and just looked at it. Well, there was not a hint of a fire; and I remember thinking to myself that since it wasn't burning, the damages would probably cost about $15,000. Always optimistic, I laughed to myself and said "Well, I just saved $35,000!" It took 30 minutes for the crash truck and crew to make it to the airplane. As the truck pulled up next to the aircraft the engine caught fire as if it had been waiting for them to get there! I began to shout for them to hurry up and spray the engine with the fire extinguisher, which they did as soon as they got out of the truck. The fire extinguishers turned out to be corrosive, and during the restoration that fact led to some expensive problems.

Eventually, everything was under control, and the fire was really out. A truck with a cherry-picker hoist arrived; and, after a quick check to make sure everything was turned off in the cockpit, they picked up the Wildcat, and the landing gear just dropped into the down position. Unfortunately, the gear wouldn't lock down, and it immediately collapsed again. Eventually, we were forced to just hoist it to a hangar. Once there, we fastened some stiffeners to hold the gear in the down and locked position. I can tell you that the kidding began almost as soon as the fire was out and everyone was assured I was okay. Even Paul Poberezny, the president of the Experimental Aviation Association, got in a free shot by suggesting that this would be an opportune time to donate the Wildcat to the EAA Museum!

Fortunately, Don Plumb had a great restoration crew based on the airport, and I left the Wildcat right there in Windsor for repairs. She didn't make it to Oshkosh that year, the only year since 1970 that I didn't have an aircraft there; but the restoration was excellent and well worth the wait. A few weeks later, I received a $25 check from Don for return fuel as he promised.

CHAPTER 14

How I Ended Up With Two Spitfires

In 1974, Ormond Haydon-Bailley, an acquaintance of mine from England, contacted me about his rather extensive collection of aircraft. He was considering selling some of them and wondered if I would be interested. I told him I might, and if he decided to sell he should let me know because I could pass along the information to warbird friends here in the U.S.

Eventually he did contact me again with a list of aircraft he had for sale; it was quite interesting. He mentioned that four Spitfires had been recently discovered in India. He said they could be purchased for $29,000 each and wondered if I might be interested. I immediately said that I would be very interested and at that price I'd take two!

Now I realize it may seem somewhat impulsive to buy two Spitfires over the phone but this is the way my logic worked: You know, after you've been paying off your home mortgage for a few years, you suddenly come to the realization that the value of the house has appreciated so much that you could sell it and make a substantial profit. Of course, since you only own one house you can't really do it. So I figured the aircraft would appreciate significantly, and if I bought two and held them for a few years, I could sell one at a significant profit that would more than cover the cost of the one I kept. It would essentially be like getting a free Spitfire!

So, it was with that reasoning that I struck a deal with Haydon-Bailley for two aircraft, and I sent him a check. He immediately began to arrange for the recovery of the aircraft in India, but before he could have them shipped back to England he was killed while flying his P-51 in France. A short while later, his brother, Wensley, called to reassure me that he was aware of the transaction and would be going to India with a Mr. Roger Sweet to bring back the aircraft.

When Wensley arrived in India it turned out there were actually nine Spitfires there. They included a fairly complete Spitfire Mark VIII which he would be keeping, three Mark 14s, and five Mark 18s. He promised me the best two of the batch. One of the Spitfires he arranged for me was somewhat incomplete, so he included an extra set of wings without telling me. When the crates arrived, there they were, sort of like a Christmas present! Over the years, as I was restoring the Spitfires, that extra set of wings served as wonderful trading material to help me obtain hard-to-find parts.

CHAPTER 15

The Japanese Zero
That Isn't

We get many questions about our Japanese Zero; it seems to fool just about everyone. In reality, the Zero is actually a highly customized fabrication built on an AT-6 airframe. It was one of a pair built to accurate specifications for the movie "Tora, Tora, Tora". They were to be used for close-up shots in the film. Of the two, this was the only one that launched from the U.S.S. Lexington during the movie. The Lexington is a well-preserved, WWII, wooden-decked aircraft carrier.

When filming was completed the aircraft returned to its Texas base and a life of air shows. My son Joe had occasion to fly it a few times when he was in Texas. So when its owner decided to sell the Zero, Joe recommended we make him an offer. We did, and he accepted. Joe flew it to our airport, and it's been active in our fleet of warbirds ever since.

We like to use the Zero in mock Airshow battles because it has both smoke and realistic machine gun sounds. To produce the gunshots, the pilot triggers a switch on the control stick which activates a mechanism that mixes two gases together then ignites them. The result is remarkably like machine gun noise. The aircraft is also fitted with a standard smoke system similar to the one installed in our Wildcat. When activated, the system injects special oil into the engine exhaust system causing a fairly dense stream of smoke out of the exhaust stack.

After the Zero mixes it up with one of the other warbirds, it eventually takes a "hit", streams smoke, and goes "down" to the applause of the crowd.

The Zero isn't the only "disguised" AT-6 in our inventory. We have an SNJ built by the U.S. Navy, which many careful observers have called an AT-6G; they're correct! The Army Air Corps sold the kits to the Navy who did the assembly, calling them SNJs. Our particular aircraft was restored by the then Head of the Department of Sociology at the University of Illinois. A true warbird enthusiast, and later Chief Flight Instructor of our own Frasca Air Services after he retired, Professor Bernie Karsh did a very accurate job of restoring the SNJ. So when he decided to put it up for sale, I couldn't see letting it leave the field; I ended up buying it, and it is also quite active in our fleet of warbirds.

CHAPTER 16

The T-34 Mentor

When we show our warbird collection to visitors, they are always somewhat overwhelmed. Needless to say, everyone wishes they could go for a ride in a warbird; we wish we could take everyone. The unfortunate fact of the matter is that most warbirds have a single seat. So we will often take them for a ride in either our T-34 or our SNJ. Both have two seats and long, glass canopies.

Unless they happen to be an antique or warbird fan, most people don't realize what it's like to purchase a warbird. You don't simply go to your local airplane dealer and buy a shiny, new warbird hot off the assembly line. These are very old and often rare aircraft. As a result, even finding an available wreck can be cause for celebration. So it was with our T-34.

We purchased our T-34 from Charlie Nogle of Tuscola, IL. Charlie has made quite a reputation over the years rebuilding and restoring T-34s. He obtained this particular aircraft as a wreck, and we quickly made him an offer, which he accepted. After moving it to our hangar, we began restoration; but pressing business considerations forced it to remain a part-time project that was shared by our mechanics over several years. Eventually, we decided that if the project was going to ever get completed, we would have to send it back down to Charlie for him to finish. Noting all our aircraft, a lot of people ask me which one I like the best. In some ways that's difficult to answer because I like them all. Each one is different; each does its own thing. One of the most significant decisions we made in the T-34 restoration process was to replace the 225 HP engine. It became a truly beautiful performing aircraft with the addition of a 285 HP engine. So, for all-around flying characteristics and general capability, I have to admit my favorite is the T-34.

On the one hand, with its 285 HP engine (and later with a 300 HP), it is easy to keep up and fly formation with our fighters at 160 knots. It handles very nicely in formation and when flying aerobatics. On the other hand, we've set it up so we could use it for cross-country flying on business trips. It has a good cruise speed combined with excellent short field takeoff and landing capability. The T-34 is probably the most versatile and easy-to-fly aircraft we own and never fail to please our customers and visitors when we take them up for a ride. It is also heavily used as a photo ship.

CHAPTER 17

Hitting It Hard
With the T-34

One of the reasons I love our little airport is because it is a real community airport in every sense. We feel as if we are its stewards and attempt to support as many different facets of general aviation as possible. One of the organizations that we welcome at Frasca Field is the Civil Air Patrol (CAP).

The CAP (of which I had been a member), is a civilian volunteer organization of the U.S. Air Force, having two primary missions: Aerospace education, and search and rescue. The CAP may be dispatched in the event of a lost aircraft or other similar situation in which the use of trained pilots and ground searchers are anticipated to be effective. CAP personnel donate their time and money to train, so we feel strongly about letting them use the airport during their exercises. So it was that one weekend I went out to the airport to do a little flying in the T-34 and noticed that the CAP was holding an exercise.

I have quite a few aircraft, some of which are very sophisticated, but the T-34 holds a special place in my heart. Ours had, at the time, the 285 horsepower modification rather than the standard 225 version because I wanted to be able to fly it alongside our P-40 and Wildcat, both of which are large and very powerful fighters. In addition to the 160 knot indicated airspeed it is able to maintain, the higher horsepower gives the T-34 very interesting short field takeoff and landing performance.

With the proper flap setting, maximum power and correct handling, we are able to lift off the runway. I then immediately level off to build up airspeed before initiating a climb. With a strong wind down the runway, the takeoff can be rather dramatic; almost like taking an elevator! The airplane is also capable of very short field landings. But high performance short field takeoffs and landing also carry somewhat of a risk because you are pushing the airplane toward the edge of its envelope and you had better be careful when you do it. Just to be safe, I like to do these maneuvers on a nice, soft grass strip; it's part of my risk management program.

On this particular day, since the CAP was having their practice search and rescue mission at Frasca Field, I decided to fly over to a friend's restricted landing area not far away. I had a good friend along for the ride, Dr. Milt Carlson, and between the two of us and with full fuel, the aircraft was at maximum gross weight. To make matters worse, it was a hot day with a gusty wind cutting through a row of trees and blowing across the runway from the left. In fact, there were also trees directly at the approach end of the runway.

I thought about the situation for a moment, considered the aircraft's short field capability, and opted to make the approach with full flaps, gear down, propeller in the fine pitch position, and holding 60 knots over the trees. Once I cleared the trees I pulled the power back, eased the nose down briefly to lose altitude, and then started to flare out. The aircraft's nose went up but physics overruled my wishes and the aircraft continued to settle rapidly.

It may not have been the best choice of approaches but the consequence of my actions didn't elude me very long. I quickly applied maximum takeoff power in an attempt to cushion the rate of descent but we hit the ground hard. The grass runway was fairly soft that particular day, something you can't tell from the air, and the nose wheel immediately dug into the ground and sheared off from the airplane. The propeller, naturally, simultaneously dug into the ground which caused a strong yawing moment that turned the airplane to the side causing both main landing gears to break. The good news was it turned out to be the shortest, short field landing I have ever made in my flying career. Had we been landing on a hard surface runway it would probably have been nothing more than a hard landing we would have laughed off. So much for landing on sod runways as a method of risk management.

Unfortunately, that was the beginning of the story rather than the end. Milt and I, shaken but uninjured, quickly exited the airplane in case of a post impact fire. However, having instinctively gone through the proper emergency procedures which include shutting off the fuel, there were no further problems. We looked over the airplane and assessed the damage noting that the propeller was bent, the left wing wrinkled, the nose cowling bent, and all three landing gears were broken off. I sighed, as we walked over to remove the headsets and some other items, and mentioned to Milt that the T-34 was one of the aircraft we self insured for hull damage. The bottom line was the expense of repair would fall squarely on my shoulders. It is interesting to note that I had a good record of not having accidents, but our insurance company would not cover the damage.

As we walked over to Frank and Rose Andrews' farm house, the owners of the private airstrip we had only recently plowed up, Milt and I made a solemn pact. We agreed we wanted to keep this quiet, especially from the press, since no one was hurt and the only damage was to my own aircraft. It was just about then we noticed that next to the airport there is a model airplane field. At the time of the accident it happens there was a radio control helicopter meet taking place. Fortunately, the T-34 was stuck in the dirt at a location on the runway that was not readily visible to the people participating in the meet, or so we thought. Ironically, we noticed a Cessna 172 flying overhead but didn't think much about it.

Frank Andrews was kind enough to drive Milt home, which was

fairly close by, and then drive me back to Frasca Field. Upon arriving at the airport I put the headsets in the trunk of my car, trying not to be too obvious that I had arrived by car and not T-34. I walked into our operations building and the first thing I heard was that an aircraft had crashed 12 miles west of us. My stomach began to churn as my worst fear was coming true. The CAP, who happened to already be airborne in a Cessna 172 on a practice mission out of my own airport, had spotted the downed aircraft. They, in turn, reported it to the local flight service station who apparently had called 911. Somewhere along the line fire engines from three communities, ambulances, and numerous police and Sheriff's Department cars got involved, not to mention the crowd from the model helicopter meets.

Sheepishly I tried to apologize to everyone and inform them that it was my airplane, everyone was fine, we had the situation under control, and we really were trying to keep the whole thing quiet. I told them the owner of the private air strip knew all about it and we agreed that by the next day I would have the airplane removed. Then I called 911 and told them that I was the pilot of the airplane reported to have crashed and that it wasn't a serious problem. "It wasn't?" she snapped back at me, "Are you aware of how many personnel and vehicles we have involved out there?"

By the next day the aircraft was removed and the only remaining casualties were my pride and the poor, broken T-34. Amazingly, after all the people that got involved, there was not a single word about it anywhere. I truly believe the local papers, radio and television stations decided aviation had enough problems as it was and didn't make an issue out it. For that, I am grateful. The T-34 was rebuilt and better than ever.

CHAPTER 18

The Italian G-46

People who know me know how proud I am of my Italian heritage, so when a friend sent me a picture of a scrapped Italian G-46 I jumped at the chance to purchase it. The poor airplane was laying in an aircraft graveyard in Milan, Italy. It was in such bad condition that I was able to arrange to have it shipped to the United States as scrap metal.

The G-46 was an Italian military training aircraft built in 1947. The best description of it would be to say it looks very similar to a T-34 with a tail wheel. It had an inverted, 225 HP Alpha Romeo engine which, for its size, made it a bit underpowered on takeoff. Once airborne, however, it has a decent rate of climb and a maximum power cruise of about 200 mph.

We decided to rebuild the aircraft with some of our own modifications. We have eliminated the front seat entirely preferring to use the rear seat to fly the aircraft. The original aircraft had a canopy that opened sideways, so that's been replaced with a more conventional sliding canopy. Perhaps the most significant alteration is replacing the 225 HP Alpha Romeo engine with a 360 HP Russian model sporting a 3-bladed prop. When completed, our G-46 looked pretty much like the WWII Italian fighter for which it was originally designed to be a trainer.

CHAPTER 19

I Don't Believe In Psychics, but I Still Missed My 40th High School Class Reunion

It was the first week of June, 1989, and I was eagerly anticipating my upcoming high school 40-year class reunion at the end of the month. On this particular weekend, however, we were holding our two day Annual Frasca Field Air Fair. It was about 11:00 A.M. on Saturday during the festivities that a good friend of mine from the local fire department accident squad showed up.

My friend told me that at a fire fighter's convention, which had taken place in town the previous week; they had a lady speaker who was a psychic. One of the things she predicted was an accident and fire that would occur at either 4:30 AM or PM, on a Sunday following a local event.

I smiled nervously and thought my friend was acting a bit odd until he explained further. He told me that a fire had occurred in a hangar on another airport that involved some rare warbird aircraft. He further said there was a man, apparently from Texas, who was travelling around the U.S. setting fire to hangars that house warbirds. Worse, he was believed to recently have been seen in our local area. Allegedly, when the event was over and there were full garbage cans in the hangar, he would throw a match into it and start a fire. My friend suddenly had my full attention.

I contacted our local Sheriff who was very supportive and assigned

Deputies to routinely patrol our grounds for several weeks. In addition, the local fire fighters set up a lookout in which we assisted. That night I made it a point to be sure that everything was locked up and secured. I also hired a private, full-time guard to patrol the property. Sunday morning I went to the airport early and stood watch myself. This vigil continued non-stop all day Sunday and Sunday night, and was repeated for the next two weekends.

After a while I began to wonder if this was all a waste of time until one day someone came into our office that made the hair on the back of my neck stand up. He asked some probing-type questions and made it a point to never face me, choosing to look in the other direction the entire time. After a few minutes he left but as he pulled away I looked at his license plate; it was from Texas! The police ran the number and discovered that the car did not belong to the man who was driving it and discovered some additional discrepancies which did not make sense. Unfortunately, the man in the car disappeared; now I was spooked.

The third weekend of June was the 40th anniversary of my high school graduation. Although I had made reservations to attend the reunion, I was so concerned about the possibility of arson that I chose to not go. I hung around the airport most of the day and evening and finally went home to bed. That Sunday morning as we awoke, there was a report on the radio about a fire that occurred in the University of Illinois' Memorial Stadium after the football game. Some students had set fire to the Astroturf!

As strange as it may sound, this satisfied the prediction made by the psychic woman at the fire fighter's convention. Suddenly, I felt relieved and everything simply returned back to normal. The man in the car was never seen again; no fire ever occurred at our airport. And while I felt bad about not having been able to attend my 40th Class Reunion, I never regretted the decision to stay and guard the hangar.

CHAPTER 20

Taking a Pass
on a PT-19

The PT-19 has touched my life on more than one occasion. My first encounter was at the beginning of my flying career when I scraped together the $20 necessary to learn to fly it despite my father's concerns. Without a doubt that first encounter left me with a positive, even nostalgic, feeling toward the aircraft. My second encounter did not live up to that memory.

After I had wrecked my Luscombe, and finally sold an Aeronca Champ, I found a PT-19 for sale near Chicago. Ravenswood Airport was about three miles north of Douglas Airport (destined to become O'Hare International). It was a really nice, little airport with a couple of grass runways and was very popular after WWII because they offered flight training under the new G.I. Bill (a war veteran's program).

I arranged to meet the owner of the PT-19 to take a look at the aircraft. The $400 asking price was certainly reasonable, but I looked it over really carefully because it was wooden. The big question, when you buy a wooden airplane, is the condition of the wood. If the airplane has been sitting outside there's always the possibility that water has seeped into it and caused rotting of the center section; a very expensive problem to fix. After a thorough inspection I was satisfied that the airplane was well cared for and a bargain. All that remained to convince me was an acceptable test flight.

The owner climbed in the front seat and I got in the back. He started her up, taxied out, warmed up the engine, revved it up a bit, taxied into takeoff position, and advanced the throttle. As we rolled further and further down the runway I began to be concerned. The two of us together weren't heavy enough to have that kind of an effect on the takeoff distance of the aircraft. I was beginning to think there must be something wrong with the engine to cause such an unusually long takeoff run. The trees at the end of the runway began to look very large when the nose of the airplane just popped up to a 45 degree climb angle!

Everything happened so fast that I couldn't judge by how much we'd cleared those trees. The big issue suddenly became the critically high nose-up angle. Instinctively I just took over the controls, pushed the nose down to recover, gently flew the pattern and landed back on the runway from which we'd just taken off. As I shut down the engine I shouted to the owner "What did you do that for?!" He turned his head around and looked at me white as a ghost and said "What did I do that for? I thought you were flying!" Frankly, I feel he just messed up.

We were both shaking visibly as we climbed out of the aircraft. Then, to our utter amazement, we saw branches and twigs embedded into the wooden wings! After looking at the damage for a moment or two he turned to me and said "You can have it for $200." Still shaking I said "No way!" and passed on the deal. As I walked back to my car I wondered to myself how many people had gotten killed in that kind of situation over the years.

CHAPTER 21

A Very Expensive Wildcat Prop

Sitting in the back of our Turbo Commander 690-B one evening on the way home from a business trip, I found myself reminiscing. As son Tom guided us back toward Frasca Field from Coatesville, PA, I let the scenery slide by my window at over 300 mph. Going Westbound produces a wonderful effect on sunsets; it does slow them down giving the viewer a longer exposure. That combined with the beauty of the flickering lights of the roads, towns, and farmhouses, brought a real surge of nostalgia out of me.

We were on our way home from a meeting with Al Sheves and his wife Pat. The Sheves owned a fixed-based operation on Chester County Airport in Coatesville, Pennsylvania. It was a wonderful mom-and-pop operation with a flight school, charter, and aircraft storage. Al was one of the first purchasers of our Frasca flight simulators in 1967. In those days we used to display our simulators at the Reading Airshow in Pennsylvania which was a very popular annual aviation business convention. Unfortunately, the Reading Airshow is no longer held, but at the time it was a place for people in the business to gather and see new equipment. Al liked the 100-F so much when he saw it at the show that he bought it right out of our display.

One reason for the current trip was to discuss replacing the old 100-F with a new Model 142 Twin Engine Simulator. In the course of our discussions I had an opportunity to look over the 100-F. To my surprise it not only looked excellent but it flew wonderfully; Al had taken very good care of that simulator. I ended up telling them I would take the old 100-F in trade, and I think that was like the frosting on the cake. But Al and I share another common interest: World War II fighter aircraft.

Al was part owner, with Jack DuPont, of a Wildcat that I tried to buy in 1967. He and I have been to, and performed in many air shows together over the years. Al has flown their Wildcat, and also various other WWII fighters. His excellent flying skills were enhanced by the fact that he was also an outstanding mechanic and aircraft restorer. Al's youthful appearance fools the casual observer but, in fact, his aviation roots go quite a bit deeper than my own; he was working on aircraft prior to WWII. You can well imagine he has many aviation contacts and is a storehouse of aviation anecdotes. As a result, I have kept in fairly regular contact with Al over the years as we try to help each other locate spare parts for the warbirds.

As Al and I were sitting there reminiscing, he reminded me of a funny conversation we had one evening over dinner at a National Aviation Trade Association Convention. As was often the case, we had been talking about locating various warbird parts when he casually mentioned that he had just obtained a Wildcat propeller. Well, that definitely caught my attention as those props are difficult to locate. I asked him where he had found it.

"Oh, some old guy named Smith in Arizona," he replied.

"John Smith?" I asked. (Not his real name)

"Yeah, that was his name. It wasn't cheap but it's in good condition" he beamed.

"I know," I said, shaking my head, "I bought it from him a couple of years ago and he's supposed to be holding on to it for me until a later date!"

Well, Al looked somewhat embarrassed by the incident until I told him how much I had paid for the prop. Then you could tell he moved from embarrassed to miffed. He'd paid twice as much as I did which meant old John had really made out on the deal. After a few minutes, Al and I had a good laugh over the whole situation. We agreed whoever needed the prop first would get it and then we would settle the whole financial mess in a manner fair to us both. Ironically, neither one of us ended up using the prop as shortly thereafter a mutual friend needed one for his Wildcat so Al sold it to him.

After the dinner conversation with Al about the prop, I called John Smith to see what he'd say if I inquired about getting it. He had some reason, which I can't recall, why he couldn't send it out right then. Subsequent calls turned up different stories each time about why he couldn't send my prop until one day he told me it had been stolen. Well, John was pretty old so it was difficult to say whether he knew better or was just running a scam. After some thought I determined, all things considered, it was easier to just let it go. Al made me out a check for what I had in it.

As Tom steered the Turbo Commander on its final descent to Frasca Field, I looked at all the beautiful lights that stood out against the darkness and thought about all the Al & Pat Sheves I know in aviation; far, far more than the John Smiths, that's for sure.

CHAPTER 22

Preserving the Past and Sharing With the Future

I am often asked why I spend so much of my time and money on the restoration of warbirds and the development of the Frasca Air Museum. It is a difficult question to answer objectively. Obviously, I enjoy flying and collecting the aircraft and associating with other like-minded people, but it is really not that simple. My interest in warbirds goes back to my childhood, long before I began flying. These aircraft are historic and need to be saved so future generations will appreciate what aviation was like during those years. The Frasca Air Museum was not so much a conscious decision to start a museum as much as it was the evolutionary result of my trying to preserve history. In addition, these aircraft are excellent investments.

There is a very dangerous period of time in the life of an airplane when it transitions from being an exciting, modern airplane to being a collectible antique. Somewhere in between, it becomes an old airplane that few are interested in any longer. Many warbirds never survived that transition and are lost forever. The desire to preserve older airplanes in general, and warbirds specifically, goes back to my youth. I have been visiting the Museum of Science and Industry in Chicago since I was 12 years old.

Dedicated to the evolution of science and technology, the Museum of Science and Industry has thousands of displays on everything imaginable but it is their aviation collection that continues to draw me back year after year. For as long as I have been going there, the museum has had a Spitfire Mark I and a German Stuka on display, side-by-side; both saw combat during WWII. The Spitfire's claim to fame is that it participated in the Battle of Britain while the Stuka fought in Africa. To this day, I still travel to the museum to look at those two aircraft but especially the Spitfire. I am so proud to have been fortunate enough to locate and restore my own Spitfires. On more than one occasion I've walked up to that Spitfire in the museum when other people have been standing around looking at it, and say "Hey, I've got one of those!" They look at me funny. Since then I added a WWII German FW190 fighter.

So after all these years, it is no surprise that I've become very involved with museums. I particularly enjoy visiting the Smithsonian which also has both a Spitfire and a Stuka on display. However, at the Smithsonian, I think my favorite display is the Wildcat with its wings folded up and placed on a simulated aircraft carrier. So when I was participating in the Experimental Aircraft Association's (EAA) annual gathering in Oshkosh, Wisconsin in 1994, I was very receptive to John Baugh's request.

Baugh, one of the Directors of Warbirds of America, asked if I would consider placing my Wildcat on a carrier display at the EAA's museum in Oshkosh. Several things immediately ran through my mind when he asked. First, I had already decided to set aside the Wildcat for restoration. Then I thought about how much I admired the display at the Smithsonian of a Wildcat with its wings folded on a carrier deck; a similar display using my aircraft at the EAA's museum was very appealing. Finally, I thought about the EAA museum in general and knew it to be truly first-class. The decision was simple: I loaned the Wildcat to the EAA for the museum display.

It wasn't the first aircraft loan I had made to the EAA; they had previously displayed one of the Spitfire's I acquired from India. Coincidentally, while my second Spitfire was on display there, they had also gotten the loan of the Smithsonian's Stuka for display. It was reminiscent of the Museum of Science and Industry and was very satisfying for me. Around the same time, I also sponsored a simulation section in their museum which included one of our old simulators as well as historic photographs of our company.

My involvement with aviation museums has not been limited to just a few major institutions. In the early 1990's, the U.S. Government began cost-cutting in the post cold war environment and shut down several military installations. One of those was Chanute Air Force Base in Rantoul, Illinois. A local committee was organized to attempt to transition Chanute to civilian use, and part of that attempt included the development of the Chanute Air Museum. I became interested in the project very early and have been an avid supporter since the beginning. We sponsor a Frasca room which displays numerous Frasca simulators ranging from the very earliest models to more modern versions. We have also included numerous historic simulation photographs, a vintage fire engine, and the cockpits of numerous airplanes and helicopters we have collected over the years. One of the most interesting displays we loaned the Chanute museum was a helicopter that belonged to the president of Italy some years ago that was also used by the Pope.

If there is any drawback to my extensive involvement in historic preservation, it may be that my family has begun to take them for granted. Warbirds and aviation collectibles have become a way of life for the Frasca family and there may be a tendency to forget they are both rare and precious. My daughter Liz, and son-in-law Graham, took their young son, Alex, to the Smithsonian's Air and Space Museum. Graham is British so the Spitfire is probably dearest to his heart, and on many occasions my grandsons have sat proudly in the cockpit of my own Spitfire. At the Smithsonian, one of the "must see" displays for my grandson was the Spitfire. Standing there, looking at it, he said he wanted to sit in it. He was told by the docent that was not possible; it is against museum rules because it is a very rare aircraft. "Well," he said, as if the rare airplane were as common as a new car, "my Grandpa lets me sit in his Spitfire!"

Grandpa said I can solo the Spitfire on my first birthday. So many endorsements, so little time...

Adventures over the years...

CHAPTER 23

The Problem with Chewing Gum

Except for ice cream sundaes and an occasional martini, I've never had much in the way of vices, and especially not smoking. But I did get into the habit of chewing gum when I'd fly. Now, you would think chewing gum was a pretty safe, healthy, and uncomplicated habit; but nothing is ever as simple as it seems. For instance, there is the time I was flying my Wildcat back from Springfield, Illinois, after routine maintenance.

It was during the early 1970s and was one of the first warm days of spring. It was a beautiful day to be flying. As I taxied out for takeoff, I unwrapped a piece of gum, stuck it in my mouth and took the runway. As always, I felt the thrill of takeoff as the Wildcat roared down the runway and climbed skyward. I leveled off at 3,000 feet and was cruising back to Champaign... Sitting there, enjoying the warmth of the sun, I was almost mesmerized by Mother Nature's effect on the ground below me as she painted patches of spring here and there.

I suddenly realized that the engine sounded rough and instinctively focused my attention on the sound of the engine; the roughness immediately stopped. After a minute or so I decided it was either my imagination or perhaps a little water in the fuel. I settled back down to enjoy the flight. Again I became aware of engine roughness, and again I concentrated intently until the boredom of nothing abnormal lulled me back to other thoughts. But each time they were interrupted by engine roughness with the same results. After several recurrences, I began to ponder what might cause me to hear something that didn't exist. Finally, I realized that every time I chewed the gum the engine sounded rough! It was the physical act of chewing that altered the way I heard the engine sound. After that, I had pretty much lost my appetite for the gum and decided to get rid of it. There was a small opening between the side of the cockpit and bottom of the canopy that seemed large enough to push the gum through. Unfortunately, and unknown to me, it was warm enough that the gum just stuck to the side of the cockpit.

The rest of the flight was uneventful, and after landing at Champaign, I went home to get ready for a flight to Glenview Naval Air Station for an Airshow. When I was ready, my wife Lucille drove me back to the airport with several of our kids in tow to watch Dad take off. I preflighted the Wildcat, started it, and taxied out to the runway. The family watched as I completed the pre-takeoff procedures, applied power and accelerated down the runway. Again, the thrill of takeoff rushed through me as the warm air washed over me through the open canopy. Shortly after lift-off I began the after-takeoff gymnastics required by the Wildcat.

The Wildcat, which has manual gear extension and retraction rather than hydraulic or electric, requires 29 turns of the crank to retract or extend the gear. The cowl flaps are also manual and then there are adjustments to the throttle, mixture and prop pitch. You get the idea. There's a lot of cleaning up to do after takeoff. Well, immediately after takeoff I glanced at the instruments and was about to adjust the power when I noticed the gum stuck to the right side of the cockpit. I pondered the gum for a second, and then with the stick in my right hand, I tried to remove the sticky substance with my left. Instinct took over at that moment, as I needed to make the appropriate after-takeoff adjustments, and my left hand went to the throttle to bring the power back to the required 36 inches of manifold pressure. Instantly, part of the gum stuck to the throttle without my realizing it. I then adjusted the prop pitch to 2300 rpm with the same hand, tacking gum to that control.

Even as I chuckled at the absurdity of the situation, I took the control stick in my left hand so I would be able to crank up the landing gear with my right. After 29 turns, the gear was up, and there was gum on the control stick. I began to laugh out loud thinking about my family watching me from below with no idea of the slapstick comedy playing out in the cockpit. Without thinking, my right hand came off the landing gear crank and took its familiar position on the control stick. Now I had gum on both hands.

I turned north toward Chicago, quickly climbed to my cruise altitude, and adjusted power with my left hand, unintentionally taking back a portion of the gum I had previously left on the throttle. Leveling off at cruise required that I trim both rudder and elevator, each of which appeared to be eager to take on some of the gum as I touched their controls. Then there were the cowl flaps to be closed and the mixture leaned; the result was an ever-more intricate spider web of gum around the cockpit.

With the canopy still open, I contemplated the situation and decided to try to bite the gum off my fingers. As I began to do so, the wind caught the strings of gum and blew them against my goggles. With my face and much of the cockpit connected by a wispy, gummy string, I decided to just close the canopy and live with the situation. Without thinking, my gum covered fingers grasped the only thing left in the cockpit without gum on it, the canopy lever.

As I flew over the beautiful Central Illinois spring scenery, I recalled the days when I had been stationed at Glenview as a TD3, the Navy's equivalent of a Staff Sergeant. It was during the Korean War and I was a LINK Trainer instructor. This was the beginning of my interest in flight simulation. Immersed in my thoughts it wasn't long before I was over Chicago and approaching Glenview Naval Air Station. I called the tower, which was anticipating the arrival of a number of warbirds for the Airshow, and was cleared to make a low pass over the field and then land.

As I taxied in from the runway I saw Bill Ross' Spitfire as well as the aircraft of numerous other friends. I was really excited as I swung the Wildcat into a tie-down spot on the ramp and shut it down. At that same moment the Base Commander, a Naval Captain, drove up in an official staff car and saluted me! He invited me to climb into the seat next to him and proceeded to thank me for coming. For the rest of the show I was extended VIP treatment; a real treat for an old Navy enlisted man.

At the conclusion of the show all the warbird pilots had their tanks topped off. The people of Glenview had arranged for 20,000 gallons of fuel for the warbirds as a way of saying thank you for coming; I only needed 39 gallons! As I taxied out for takeoff my thoughts were filled with many memories. I was thankful to be involved with such a wonderful group of people, all dedicated to keeping those old warbirds flying and landing my Wildcat on Glenview.

CHAPTER 24

The '46 Luscombe on Skis

Sometimes you have to know what's on a man's mind to understand why he does something that seems dumb. Champaign was engulfed in cold weather one day as my son Tom and I flew to Florida on business. As we were wrapping up the next day, our host said, "Why don't you stay around a few more days and enjoy the sunshine and warm weather? They got a deep blanket of snow in Champaign last night." I replied, "That's exactly why I want to go back!" Now, to a Floridian, that sounds pretty silly, but it happened that I had a 1946 Model 8A Luscombe on skis that had been waiting for just such an occasion. This one I bought for $7,500 in 1990.

The little Luscombe was almost identical to the one I owned in the early '50s. In those days, I flew her with the enthusiasm of a young pilot looking forward to adventure. I was every bit as enthusiastic to fly her later, as I looked back with nostalgia and appreciation for a fine, little airplane. The engine had recently been overhauled by Dale Rapp, our chief mechanic, and was one of the smoothest small, piston engines I have ever flown.

So, it was late that Saturday night when Tom and I found ourselves bucking a 55 miles per hour headwind enroute to Champaign. Fortunately, we were in our Turbo Commander and still able to make a ground speed of about 215 miles per hour. As we moved into the

Midwest, we began to see traces of snow on the ground which steadily increased until literally everything on the ground was covered with beautiful, soft, white snow. As always, it was good to be home – especially with the snow.

The next morning was Sunday, and after church my son, David, and I went to the airport and pulled the Luscombe out of the hangar and onto the snow. I climbed into the familiar seat as David propped it for starting. With eager anticipation I called out "contact!" and David pulled the prop through from behind while standing on the right ski; the engine roared to life. Because it was so cold, the skis had already frozen to the snow; so David wiggled the wings to break the skis loose, and I gave it sufficient throttle to get it moving forward before it would have a chance to freeze to the snow again. As I taxied away, David was already preflighting the T-34 to do some flying of his own.

The cold temperature, combined with about 10 inches of snow to support the skis, made the Luscombe complete its takeoff roll in short order. With so many aviation friends in Central Illinois who own their own restricted runways, I just wandered from one friend's runway to another, making a low pass here or a touch-and-go landing there. The countryside was blanketed in beautiful, white snow, and most of the airports I visited had not been used since the snow fell. It was just simply a beautiful day to fly. Eventually, I worked my way back to Frasca Field where I landed and taxied up to Lucille's Flying School and Hot Dog Stand. When the engine sputtered to a stop, I climbed out, put a blanket over the engine to keep it warm, and noticed that my Sunday lunch-bunch had begun to arrive at the airport.

Our more-or-less regular Sunday lunch group flies a wide array of airplanes. We have some slick, new ones, some vintage models, and warbirds. What we all have in common is a love of aviation, the enjoyment of swapping stories, and the unshakable belief that the food at the Bloomington, Illinois Arnies restaurant is the best in the world after a Sunday morning flight. On the way home several of us practiced formation flying and I couldn't help reflecting on how lucky I was to have such a good group of friends. All too soon the wintery countryside had slipped away, and there was Frasca Field straight ahead. We made our usual low pass over the airport, pitched out, landed and taxied to the ramp.

As we shut down our engines, I noticed my daughter, Liz, and son-in-law, Graham, with their baby Alexander, walking up. They were visiting for a few days. Graham, whose slight build is a contrast to my own more substantial stature, had already figured out our combined weights in his head. He walked up and casually said, "Hey, I think you and I could get that Luscombe airborne." He was clearly eager to go for a ride so I climbed in and fired her back up. I told him he would have to stand outside and hold a wing tip while I made a 180 degree turn so we would be facing toward the runway. Turning a plane on skis in the snow from a dead stop is often difficult. He did so, and once the turn was complete, Graham climbed aboard and began to settle in. Unfortunately, the deep snow was fairly soft, and despite going to full power, the airplane simply wouldn't budge.

"Don't get too comfortable," I shouted to Graham, "you're going to have to climb back out, wiggle the wings to get the skis to break loose from the snow, then jump back in as the aircraft starts to move forward!" The smile on his face as he rocked the wings and jumped back into the moving airplane showed it was as big an adventure for him as it was for me. As we approached the end of runway 27, which is normally our west sod runway, I was looking for traffic and finishing up the preflight check. Wanting to avoid the possibility of getting stuck in the snow, I didn't slow down; I just kept adding power as I pointed the nose of the Luscombe down the runway. But there wasn't all that much power to add as it took a substantial amount just to taxi through the deep and often drifted snow with the extra weight. She would alternately lunge across areas of flat, crusted snow then lurch to one side or the other as she would valiantly plow through random snow drifts. After sliding or perhaps "being dragged" is a better term, down the runway for about 3000 feet, our airspeed was barely 25 miles per hour. As I watched a flock of small birds pass me on the runway, I decided it was time to abort the takeoff and re-evaluate the situation.

As I taxied back down the runway I glanced at Graham, whose smile continued to reflect a trust in both pilot and machine, and said, "We'll just taxi back for another go at it. Hopefully, we'll get more speed if we latch onto our own tracks in the snow." We didn't. We alternately strained against our seatbelts and were pushed back against our seats as the airspeed indicator stubbornly refused to go beyond 25 miles per hour. Increasing oil temperature and decreasing oil pressure indications, combined with an ever-so-slight tightening of Graham's smile, clearly confirmed my evaluation of the situation: Time to go back.

After shutting down the engine in front of Lucille's Flying School and Hot Dog Stand, I opened the cowling and checked the oil: a quart low. By the time I got a quart of slightly heavier weight oil with expectations of getting a higher oil pressure, and poured it into the engine, the engine had cooled off a bit. I wanted to make sure there weren't any problems so I said, "Graham, let me give it a try alone". After start-up, a brief engine check and taxi, I proceeded to attempt another takeoff run but this time alone. The little airplane lurched and lunged once more down the runway but this time after only a bit more of a roll than normal it lifted off the waves of snow into its natural environment; the aircraft was truly a joy to fly.

After some air work and touch-and-goes, I was satisfied that her performance was fine; she just couldn't handle Graham's extra weight while trying to plow through the snow. So I flew back to Frasca Field, landed, taxied back to the hangar, and shut her down. Getting her into the hangar on skis was another matter. Dale, clever guy that he is, built a set of cradles with wheels to put over the skis so you could move the airplane on a concrete surface. While they were an engineering marvel to build and use, he didn't take into account the effect of aging on the pilot; someone had to lift up each ski and someone had to place it in the cradle. Graham, now long since dried off and warm, once more ventured into the cold to assist. As I lifted each wing, he attached the cradle to the ski. My back barked every time I thrust the airplane upward, but before long she was sitting on wheels. We then pushed her back into the hangar and returned to the warmth of Lucille's Flying School and Hot Dog Stand. The next morning Graham was chuckling about the adventure and said, "Wait until I tell my airline friends". I laughed with him as I rubbed my aching back and inquired whether any of them were also chiropractors.

CHAPTER 25

The Great
Alaskan Adventure

A friend contacted me one day and offered to sell me a 1946 Piper PA-12. The original version had a 100 hp engine with a single seat in front and a two-person bench seat in the back. This particular aircraft, however, had been upgraded to a 135 hp engine and had the big tundra tires. It was a very nice combination for flying off grass or other unimproved airstrips. He wanted $1,750 which was a good buy even though it was in pieces and not currently in flying condition. I took him up on the offer.

We arranged for the PA-12 to make the 25-mile ground journey to Champaign where it was stored in the back building of our old factory. It was in good company as there was also a wrecked T-34 and the two, newly arrived Spitfires from India; they too were in pieces. We began stripping the PA-12 down in our spare time. Before long, we were given a proposal from someone in Iowa who quoted a very fair price for a full restoration of the aircraft. The job would include a recently overhauled 150 hp engine, and configuration appropriate for bush flying. We agreed and arranged for the aircraft to be shipped to Iowa. About 18 months later the airplane was returned; they had done a very nice job and it flew really well. We kept the airplane around for several years until Joe asked to take it up to Alaska to do some serious bush flying.

Joe became somewhat of an Alaskan pilot "Jack-of-all-trades." For instance, he used to haul fish with the PA-19. He once showed me a receipt he had for hauling 1100 pounds of fish off a beach, in the PA-12! Fishing is a major industry in Alaska and Joe made a living in a number of ways involving them. He would fly out over the ocean looking for silver salmon and when he'd find a school he'd report it to the fishing boats. They would travel over to where the school was located and drop their nets. Joe would get a percentage of the profit, which could easily run into thousands of dollars, for finding them.

Probably as much as anything, Joe loved the Alaskan wilderness. He used to fly fishermen and hunters into remote, inaccessible areas and guide them on fishing and hunting trips. He began to develop quite a reputation for bush flying and was eventually contracted by someone to go into the bush, pick up a downed airplane, and restore it for an agreed upon amount. The airplane he was to get was a Piper Super Cub and it was located in about as inaccessible an area as you can imagine.

Joe studied the problem for some time and it appeared he would either have to load it onto a raft and float it down river or wait until winter and sled it out. Neither prospect appealed to him very much so he finally decided he'd cut the fuselage into three pieces and load them one-by-one onto a single engine Otter aircraft and fly it out. The wings had to be strapped on either side of the fuselage which, I'm sure, made for interesting aerodynamics.

After several trips, and a lot of hard work, Joe had all the pieces of the airplane in a garage adjoining his apartment. He then began the task of restoration. It took a very long time but he finally got the job done in a first class manner. Later, when asked about the recovery and restoration, he would laugh and say he figured he made about $1.50 an hour on the project but that it was certainly quite an experience.

At one point, while Joe was still in Alaska, I had occasion to do some business with Anchorage Community College. It was an excellent opportunity to visit Joe and also get a tour of that part of Alaska.

I was absolutely fascinated with the area as we drove out to Lake Hood where Joe kept the PA-12; I couldn't wait to get airborne and see it from above. I was astounded at the huge number of both land and sea planes that were based there. I found out that Alaska has more airplanes per capita than any other state and it seemed as if they were all right there at Lake Hood!

It was great being in the PA-12 again. On the way to the airport Joe asked if I'd like to fly up to an island with him the next day. He said it would give me a first-hand view of Alaska. I readily accepted just to spend time with him and to see Alaska close up. As we climbed out after takeoff, Joe said he was going to give me a bush flying lesson. He told me most of Alaska is inaccessible due to lack of roads. Travelers either go on foot, by water, or by airplane, the latter being preferred. Unlike other states, in Alaska you may legally land just about anywhere you can outside of incorporated areas.

After a few minutes we arrived over a river with a narrow, flat, clear shoreline. Joe then demonstrated takeoffs and landings on the river bank. At the conclusion of one landing he jumped out of the airplane and told me to give it a try while he waited on the ground. I was a little rusty on PA-12 technique, and it felt somewhat uncomfortable landing under those conditions, but all things considered I did a pretty good job. I was really excited as Joe climbed back into the airplane for the short trip back to Lake Hood.

It was an early call the next morning and, after a hearty breakfast, we made it to the airport while there was still a real chill in the air. It was to be my great Alaskan adventure! Joe put his rifle in the PA-12 then pulled considerable survival gear out of the car and put it in too. I guess it hadn't hit home where we were going. I was still thinking in terms of our little expedition to the river the day before - close enough to the city that we could have hiked back for dinner if necessary. I was about to discover that the previous day was the exception to the rule. In Alaska, you are almost never near a population center; the survival skills and equipment necessary to live for an extended period in the wilderness can easily be the difference between life and death. This trip would be 125 miles away!

Before long we were airborne and within minutes I began to realize the reality of bush flying. As the town slid away behind us there were some scattered cabins for a few miles and then nothing. There were no cabins, no roads, not even a possible landing site, just trees and rivers. From our vantage point of a few thousand feet, there was no sign that would indicate any intelligent life on this planet; it was an uncomfortable feeling. After a while I asked Joe if we were getting close. I must have seemed like a little boy on vacation but he chuckled and said we were about one-quarter of the way. I was getting a bit anxious at the prospect of continuing for that much longer over such inhospitable terrain as I hadn't seen what I would consider a safe place to land since we left the airport. I was beginning to wonder if there was any intelligent life in our little PA-12. Clearly, this was not like flying in Illinois!

The PA-12 somehow felt smaller than I had remembered as I sat there alternately feeling comforted by my faith in Joe's ability and judgment, and discomforted by looking at the ground. As if an emotional magnet, the safety of the airport kept me wishing we would turn back. After what seemed an eternity, Joe announced we were about halfway to our destination; we had passed what trans-oceanic pilots call "the point of no return". It was now closer to go to the destination than back to the point of origin. Knowing he had a safe landing site in mind at our destination, the emotional magnet instantly reversed polarity, Lake Hood forgotten, the island suddenly became very important!

We finally arrived. Joe circled it once then descended to about 50 feet above the ground and flew up and down the beach looking for deer. Although we were more than 100 miles from even the slightest hint of civilization, I was shocked to see the garbage that had washed ashore from the sea. As I was contemplating the concept of man verses the environment, feeling really comfortable for the first time since we left, I was jarred back to reality. Joe had spotted a deer and landed on a section of the beach closest to where it was foraging.

Joe jumped out of the airplane, grabbed his rifle and quickly but quietly set out in a direction that would take him to the area where he had spotted the deer. I climbed out and hurried to catch up. Suddenly, there was the deer but Joe hadn't spotted him yet. Until that moment I didn't realize exactly what we were about to do. I looked at that deer, did a quick mental weight and balance calculation, and then briefly pondered exactly how we'd fit such a huge animal into our little airplane. I didn't much care for the idea of having a dead dear sitting on my lap for a couple of hours. So, with little more thought, I literally shouted, "Joe, there it is!" Joe's head swiveled toward the deer whose head swiveled toward us only a fraction of a second before it took off running; the forest swallowed up the deer within a second.

On the way back to the airplane I tried to reason with Joe. "There's no way that deer would fit in the airplane with us," I said. He didn't seem particularly swayed by that comment and it wasn't until later that he'd show me the ticket saying he'd hauled 1,000 pounds of Salmon in that same little PA-12. Well, as luck would have it, the airplane got bogged down on the beach. Joe explained it wasn't uncommon for that sort of thing to happen and the solution was for him to get in the airplane and fire it up while I attempted to help rock it free from the outside. The method worked but Joe didn't stop, he just took off and left me standing on the beach! Suddenly, I wondered just how angry he was about that deer! I also had the profound realization there was no way I could get back to civilization making the importance of survival gear crystal clear in my mind. Joe, of course, had no such thought in his mind. He simply circled and landed the airplane on a different part of the beach that was firm enough to hold the weight of the airplane and both of us.

On the trip back to Lake Hood I thought a lot about life in Alaska.

While I'd known for years that Joe's flying ability and judgment were in a league of their own, I gained even greater respect for him that day. My apprehensions had dissolved and it was a beautiful flight back. When I think back to that trip to Alaska the only words I can summon to describe it properly are: It was fantastic!

CHAPTER 26

Lucille Learns To Fly

I have always enjoyed air shows but it was the purchase of the Wildcat in 1968 that really got me heavily involved. From that point on I began attending a lot of shows every summer. I recall one year, while attending the Hamilton, Ontario, Canada Airshow that I began to have more than a flicker of concern about all the time I was spending away from my family although I often had my children attend. Joe would fly them over in our Mooney. Later the rest would fly over as they got their licenses.

At that point I had probably attended the Hamilton Airshow for about fifteen consecutive years or so. One of the primary reasons I went was because some good friends of mine have a museum there: The Canadian Warplane Heritage Museum. I was flying the P-40 that weekend and Joe had the Wildcat. It occurred to me it was the Saturday before Father's Day and I thought maybe I should really be home with my wife. By then, the kids were pretty well raised and off doing their own things.

So I mentioned to Dennis Bradley, who was in charge of the Airshow, that I would like to leave that afternoon to be home for Father's Day. He sort of winced a bit, hating to see the P-40 leave early, but understood how I felt and agreed. As planned, I took off during the early afternoon and headed West toward Detroit. After clearing customs in Detroit, I called Lucille to tell her the happy news: Dad will be home for Father's Day!

"Fine, Rudy" she said, "but I won't be home!" "What?" I said, shocked. "Well Rudy, did you think I'd just be just sitting around here while you're off at air shows? I've got things to do." she said matter-of-factly. Talk about a letdown! I guess all these years I had pictured her sitting at home, anxiously waiting for me to return and tell her of my adventures. Talk about a rude awakening. Since that day I have dramatically reduced the number of days I spend away from home. I might fly to an Airshow for a day, but I get back home quickly now.

Over the years, just about everyone in the family learned to fly except my oldest daughter Mary, who had no interest in flying at all, and Lucille. After buying the airport, however, Lucille decided it was time to see what flying was all about and started taking lessons. She meticulously worked through the whole program including ground school and flight training.

I remember on one of her solo cross countries she didn't want me to know when she was going because she was afraid I would follow her. She was right, of course, as I would have wanted to make sure she didn't get lost. Well, she managed to keep me from finding out about it and took off on a scheduled, cross country trip to Kankakee, Illinois, that she and her flight instructor worked out. Kankakee was an ideal student pilot cross country destination because it had a very nice airport about 80 miles almost directly North of Frasca Field.

Quite a while later she called me at the factory and said she had gotten a little bit lost, was okay, knew where she was, had refueled, checked the weather and would be flying back soon. Casually, I asked where she was calling from, and just before hanging up she said, "Appleton, Wisconsin. Bye Rudy." "Appleton, Wisconsin?" I shouted into a dead telephone, "That's 300 miles north of here!" She was actually back at our airport.

Despite her getting a "little bit lost" that one time, I was really proud of Lucille. She just kept working hard at her lessons until she finished and passed her private pilot check ride. The family presented her with a beautiful plaque that had her picture on it and the inscription "Flying Mom of the Year." It was some time later, however, that I knew Lucille had really taken to flying. The boys and I were at an Airshow and I called home to say hello and was told that she and Liz had left for the day; they had flown to a fly-in breakfast somewhere. It was pretty clear that if there was going to be any knitting done in our house, I would have to be the one to learn how.

CHAPTER 27

Flying the Blenheim at Duxford

John Dibbs and John Romain, two friends from Duxford Airport in England, visit us about every six months or so to do some air-to-air photography for various calendars, magazines, and books.

John Romain is an accomplished pilot, and John Dibbs is a very fine photographer. Often my aircraft are used for his photographs. My Spitfire and P-40 have appeared in John's calendar, "Flying Legends", and the SNJ and T-34 have been camera ships. We usually have a great time while they are out here. When we go to England, it is usually reciprocated. But this trip to England I had in the middle of May 1998 was to attend the Royal Aeronautical Society symposium in London to be awarded a silver medal for Frasca's work in simulation. However, wishing to make the most of the trip, I arrived a few days early to spend some time at Duxford. It is a fascinating museum field, and also very active. Duxford was a Royal Air Force base back in the 1930s, then during the war saw first RAF fighters then USAAF fighters based there. It is now home to the Imperial War Museum and various collections of airworthy warbirds.

John Dibbs had some excellent contacts with British Airways and obtained business class tickets for my Chicago to London Heathrow trip. I arrived Friday morning and planned on spending the rest of the day and the following day at Duxford. Dibbs had specifically told me to bring my flight suit. When I got there and met the two Johns, it was mentioned that we would be flying over to North Weald, a former RAF base where there was to be an air show that weekend. North Weald and Duxford were both important Battle of Britain airfields.

In addition to flying many war birds, John Romain's business is running a maintenance and restoration shop at Duxford. He does some beautiful restorations. One of the aircraft he has restored is a twin-engine WWII Blenheim bomber – a very rare aircraft. Actually, when I bought my two Spitfires from Ormand Hayden-Bailey 25 years previously, I came close to buying some of the aircraft parts that were used to build another Blenheim. It was later very sadly wrecked. John picked up what pieces he could from that, and together with some others, beautifully restored the Blenheim I was to fly in.

The Blenheim, which was built about 1935, was faster than the fighter aircraft of the time. They were, of course, mainly bi-plane types. When the Hurricane, Spitfire, and ME-109 came along, the Blenheim was by comparison slow. However, it did play a very important part in the early part of WW II.

John also had access to a Lysander. It, too, was a very famous and important aircraft during WW II. It was a rather large, single-engine aircraft using the same power plant as the Blenheim and the Bristol Mercury making it very slow. It was ideal for landing in very short fields. It was used in covert operations overseas where pilots would fly in and drop off or pick up spies or rescue people from fields in France or Belgium. Such operations were often conducted at night making them all the more difficult and dangerous.

I spent the remainder of Friday just visiting the various hangars and museums at Duxford. I had a good dinner, slept well, and then arrived early Saturday morning to see what Dibbs and Romain had in store for me. It turns out they had some fantastic plans; but first I looked over John's shop to see what aircraft he was working on at the time. There was a T-6, very similar to my SNJ, and another Blenheim cockpit that had been modified to be used as a car. Romain was bringing it back to its proper configuration so it could be used on another Blenheim aircraft.

John Romain also had two very rare and historic German fighters – the ME-109 aircraft. One was Black Six, a 109-G, and had been previously beautifully restored but had been in a recent accident and was being prepared for restoration again. And next to it was a 109E that had fought in the Battle of Britain.

When I first flew my Spitfire at Duxford in 1992, it was planned to have a formation flight with my Spitfire and Black 6. Air vice Marshall John Allison would have flown Black 6 with me in my Spitfire, and we would have flown over the White Cliffs of Dover. After I had completed my initial flying in the Spitfire, the weather turned bad and we were running short of time, so we couldn't get that flight in our schedule. I've always been a little sad because of it.

The boys were preparing for a flight to the former RAF base of North Weald for the air show on the following day. However, they were doing flying prior to the trip, and Romain suggested that I put my flight suit on. We then went to the Blenheim which was already prepared and ready for a local flight in the Duxford-Cambridge area. He said, "Follow me on in," which was more easily said than done.

It isn't the easiest of things to get into a Blenheim. First, you use foot and hand holds to climb up the fuselage behind the left wing, swinging onto the wing and standing up, before walking along the top of the fuselage to the cockpit canopy where you lower yourself through the open canopy. Romaine was less than half my age and climbed right up there and on in; and he is also a bit smaller. Then my turn came. I can honestly say that is the most difficult airplane that I have ever entered. But it was one of the most fascinating and most historic aircraft that I have had a chance to fly in.

As I said, I almost bought quite a few of the pieces that were to become part of this aircraft 25 years earlier. That was when I closed the deal on two Spitfires, and the Blenheim components were available. So now it was great to be getting close to, and into, this aircraft.

I got myself belted in alongside of John, and I must admit it was a bit of a tight fit. I couldn't help but note the beauty of the inside of the aircraft: the instrument panel, the controls, everything. It was better than new condition. Inasmuch, the Bristol-Mercury engines, were radials and they had to be manually pulled through to eliminate the oil that usually settles down in the lower cylinders. John had made sure that the ignition switches and the instrument controls were in the proper position so that the engines wouldn't fire; then the props were pulled through by the ground crew.

With the wheels properly chocked so that the aircraft wouldn't move forward, the man who had pulled the prop through then obtained a fire extinguisher; and when John called, "clear," he acknowledged clear, and John started the engines. As in most round engines, it spit and sputtered a bit, then caught and started with a deep- throated roar with the smoke billowing from the stacks. John then started the procedure for the other engine. After the engine was cleared out and started running properly, John called to have the chocks removed, and we taxied out toward the runway.

The Bristol-Mercury engines are very sensitive and have to be warmed up, and the throttles have to be moved slowly because of the peculiarities of the carburetor system. Open up too fast, and you get a rich cut. After about ten minutes of warming up and proper checkouts, he asked if I was ready for takeoff, which I promptly said I was; and we did. It was one of the most exhilarating experiences I have ever had.

I was in an aircraft that was designed and built back in the '30s when the fastest fighters that the British had were bi-planes. It was named after Blenheim Palace where Churchill was born and raised. Incidentally, Blenheim Palace is very close to CSE, our agents that are located in near-by Oxford. In fact, the school was called the Oxford Air Training School.

We took off from the grass and got airborne in a decent roll because we really had no load to speak of, and made a turn toward nearby Cambridge. For those who don't know, Cambridge is an old quaint town, with one of the oldest universities in the world. Many pictures have been taken of Cambridge from the air; however, I doubt if any have been taken of Cambridge from a Blenheim probably since World War II and very unlikely by an American. I made it a point to get the distinguishing features of the Blenheim in the picture.

Although there were no controls available to me from the bench I was sitting on, John did make the offer to me to reach over and fly the Blenheim, which I did. The feel and response of the control wheel was nothing unusual and was correctly consistent with the aircraft I had been flying over the years. After about 15 minutes I suggested to John that we return to Duxford. I knew that he had quite a few things to do before he brought the Blenheim over to North Weald. He made a low pass over the runway, then came around and landed on the grass. I took quite a few pictures as we were doing so. I was impressed with how well John flew the Blenheim knowing that he also restored the aircraft and knew the systems. There was no question in my mind that if an emergency came up, he would be able to handle it very skillfully. After we landed, John taxied over to the parking area, and amidst the clicking of many cameras, shut it down. Now the problem was getting back out of the Blenheim by reversing the procedure. But that was a little easier.

The excitement, however, wasn't over for the day. Dibbs and Romain had other things in store and said to hang on to the flight suit. While Romain was preparing to fly the Blenheim over to North Weald and take care of some other checkouts, Dibbs and I drove over to North Weald airport and had a great conversation en-route. He had mentioned that we would either drive or fly to another airport down south, but I didn't quite understand what was going on. I thought perhaps he was going to do some air-to-air photography, and he just wanted me to come along and watch, which I was happy to do.

We arrived at the North Weald base where they were planning an air show, and I found the field quite fascinating. It was an ex-RAF base, as I mentioned earlier, and many of the show aircraft were flying in. I had a chance to meet many new and interesting people and see some of the interesting aircraft that were inside hangars as well as out. I noticed the Lancaster, a very rare Mark II Spitfire, and a Hurricane of the Royal Air Force's Battle of Britain Memorial Flight which had flown in to take part in the show. A little later a C-54 arrived that had just flown in from the U.S. and was ready to partake in the 50th anniversary of the Berlin Airlift.

Romaine had arranged to have a Staggerwing Beech, a very rare antique aircraft, fly us to a field in south England; however, the aircraft wasn't available. A couple hours later a Piper Twin Engine Seneca flew in from another field, and we loaded aboard and took off for the flight. However, after we got airborne we heard a loud air noise. One of the latches of the door was not secure. We continued on trying to close the door, but it didn't work. There was an airport directly beneath us, so we landed there, shut the engine down, secured the door, and took off again. This was another interesting airport, Stapleford Tawney. It had been a satellite field to North Weald during the Battle of Britain.

The route took us over a good part of London. It is a very historic area because this was where the main Battle of Britain had taken place. We continued on, and in about a half-hour we were circling a grass field. I could see a two-place Spitfire sitting by one of the hangars with some people looking up at us. Dibbs asked, "Do you have any idea what is happening?" and I said, "Yep, there is a two-place Mark IX, and I believe I'm going to get a ride in that and a good chance that we are going to be flying over the White Cliffs of Dover." Dibbs said, "That's what it's all about." I had spoken of the failed plan to get Black 6 and my Spitfire over the White Cliffs.

We landed at Goodwood, which had also been a Battle of Britain airfield, and the home of a famous motor racing circuit of the 1950's and 60's. As we landed, the Spitfire was being taxied over to the refueling area and it was filled up. So John and I walked over, and there was Norman Lees who was going to be taking me up in the aircraft. Norman was the pilot who flew the Yak 11 as a camera ship in England when I had been flying my Spitfire. John Dibbs in the backseat of the Yak 11 took some great air-to-air photography. For a living he flew with Virgin Atlantic Airlines. I looked over the aircraft, especially the backseat, and couldn't help but note that the back seat was a bit smaller than I was used to, but that didn't hold me back from putting on my chute and climbing in and getting myself buckled up. Norman then put his chute on, climbed in the front seat, buckled up, and with the help of the ground crew handling chocks, Norman started the aircraft. My Spitfire is the only Spitfire I have flown, so I looked forward to flying another, especially one that did not have the more powerful Rolls Royce Griffin in it.

This Mark IX was used in the Normandy Invasion, and it also had a history that was quite interesting. It did shoot down two and a half German aircraft during World War II. The half, of course, means one shared with another pilot. It was modified from single-place to two-place for the Irish Air Force after WW II. This was so it could be used as a trainer as it had controls in both cockpits.

We took off, circled the field, and joined up then flew formation with the Piper Seneca that we had flown over in. John Dibbs was busy taking pictures of the Spitfire. We then peeled off and just flew around the area for a while looking at some of the very historic scenery, Norman handed control over to me to do the flying. For some reason we just forgot to fly over to the White Cliffs of Dover, so that part is still lacking.

Norman flew back to the airport, made a low pass and came around and was going to land, but gave it power and went around again. Then he came in to land the second time, taxied in, and shut it down. It had been a great experience. I asked Norman why he went around. He said that was the third flight he had in that particular Spitfire since it was restored. The first was with no one in the rear seat, the second was with a 140 pounder, and the third was with me; and with the chute, I had to be in the area of 260 pounds which, obviously became a bit of a problem because of the rear center of gravity. The Spitfire is very sensitive in this respect. Norman mentioned that it just didn't feel right in the first approach, but then knew what to expect on the second.

Spitfires were not designed for a fuel tank behind the cockpit; however, they did need to add more fuel as the aircraft flew from England to Europe. They did add a rear tank; but the pilot had to be very careful taking off and using up the fuel in this tank before entering into combat. My particular aircraft, the Mark XVIII with the Rolls Royce Griffin was designed to accommodate the rear tanks. After thanking Norman for taking me up in the Spitfire, I mentioned I hoped to reciprocate when he comes to the U.S., which is planned for the following month. He is a very experienced pilot.

We climbed back into the Seneca and proceeded to fly back to North Weald. However, North Weald closed at 7 p.m., and this was after 7, so we landed at Stapleford where we had landed previously on the way to south England. The owner of the Seneca had driven over to the airport to pick us up and to drive us back to North Weald where we would get John's car. On the way, David, who had flown the Seneca, mentioned, "Rudy, I have been trying to buy one of your simulators." I said, "What is going on here?" He said he needs both a helicopter and a fixed-wing simulator. So I donned my cap as president of Frasca International, the manufacturer of simulators, and discussed this.

Upon arriving at North Weald we found out that they were having a party for the air show people, and we were invited. So, we had a chance to meet more great people including the crew that flew in the C-54 from the U.S., and that Saturday turned out to be a very eventful day. I stayed at the Duxford Lodge which is a very quaint and popular hotel. During World War II it was the Base Commander's home.

Duxford Lodge is on the outskirts of Duxford Airport and is its closest hotel. It has a great restaurant and it is best that you make reservations if you plan on staying there for dinner. John Dibbs, as usual, picked me up in the mornings. We had breakfast together and planned the day's activities. So after an 8 a.m. breakfast, we drove to the airport to find John Romain and his pilots and mechanics having a meeting to determine who would be flying the additional aircraft that they had to take over to North Weald. While we were waiting for John and his people to complete their meeting, I looked over some interesting projects that he had, and chatted with a gentleman from South Africa who is also a Spitfire owner. In fact, he was the only Spitfire owner in South Africa at the time.

Two of the aircraft that were awaiting restoration were the 109s I mentioned. One was a 109E which actually flew in the Battle of Britain and even had gun holes in it. The other was the 109G, called Black Six, which was involved in an accident the year before. The 109E would be restored for strictly museum use, and the 109G was expected to be restored to fly again. John was also restoring a Blenheim cockpit section that had been modified for use as a road vehicle for quite a few years.

So with the meeting over, John came out and said, "Put on your flight suit. We are going to be flying to North Weald now." As I went out to the field there was the Lysander, which I expected to be flying in, and also the German Storch which is another very rare short field aircraft. John had mentioned that I would be flying the Storch. It also a very rare aircraft and one that I was very interested in flying. However, my heart was set on the Lysander. I mentioned, "John, I have quite a few more years to go, and I look forward to flying the Lysander one of these days." John said, "Well, if you can get into it, you can fly it." I guess he saw the problems I had climbing up into the Blenheim and thought I would have the same problems with the Lysander. I said, "No, that's no problem. It's about the same way I get up in the Wildcat," which I promptly showed him. He said, "Okay, get in."

I climbed up in the back seat of the Lysander and looked in. It was a very cavernous cockpit with no controls. In fact, all it did have was a barstool-type seat which was canvas covered. This is the aircraft that they used to fly at night to France or Belgium or wherever to drop off spies or pick them up. So it has a big area in back where they would put the people in, because it would take more than one in many cases.

I climbed in by stepping on the seat. Lee Proudfoot, the pilot, climbed in the front seat. I put on the helmet, plugged it in, and found the communications between us was very adequate. Lee gave me a briefing on the flight, what to expect, where we were going, the path we were taking, and mentioned if the engine quit, we would obviously have to land in the best field we could find; and he said to be prepared to flip over after landing. I kind of thought to myself that this was interesting, but I really wanted to fly in this aircraft.

There were some structural bars right in front of me. I thought I would just wrap my arms around them and clasp my hands for the take-off and landing. That would serve as my shoulder straps. The Lysander has the same Bristol-Mercury engine that the Blenheim has, and with all its peculiarities. Lee got the engine started, and we again went into a long warm-up procedure because it was spitting and sputtering as he gave throttle to it, so he just warmed it up that much more. He advanced the power very smoothly to make sure it wouldn't cut out on him. He then lined up with the grass runway and took off. The airplane just took a very short run to be airborne.

It was a fascinating 30-minute flight to North Weald. Upon arrival, we made a low pass and had a chance to look things over and then land. Lee taxied to the show area, and we parked next to the Blenheim alongside a fence. There were many people awaiting the aircraft, and the Lysander was quite an attention-getter. Although I had flown into many air shows in the US and Canada, this was the first Airshow I had flown into in an exhibition aircraft in another country. I spent the rest of the day watching the Airshow and meeting some old friends and also meeting new friends. We all had intense interest in these World War II aircraft and had much to talk about.

There were many interesting acts including Carolyn Grace flying her two-place Spitfire. We then met Charlie Brown who had been one of the test pilots on my Spitfire and who checked me out in it. He and Romain flew a dual act in the two Spitfires. It was really something to see. Later, Lee Proudfoot flew the Lysander with Romain flying the Blenheim. They made numerous formation low passes, and I didn't have my camera with me! Stephen Grey showed up with his AD4 and did a great aerobatic routine. That man has a lot of talent. Then there were low passes by the Battle of Britain Memorial Flight including the Lancaster, Mark II Spitfire, and the Hurricane. It was very exciting to see all this history flying by.

The DC-4 that arrived the day before made a very interesting flight as part of the 50th Anniversary of the Berlin Airlift. This was the first of its many visits to airfields for the 50th Anniversary. At the end of the day, Geoff Hughes showed up with his car, and we drove on to London where we would be attending the Royal Aeronautical Society Symposium on Low-Cost Simulation where I would give a talk.

Rudy in the early days as an instructor.

Receiving the NATA Award.

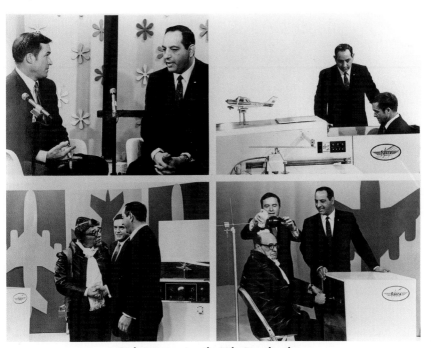

Rudy as a guest on the Mike Douglas show.

Rudy's First Luscombe (age 22)

Rudy with one of his first simulators.

Ready to fly the P-40!

With an early model and the first Frasca Full Flight Simulator. Customer for the FFS was the Indonesian Air Force. This sale led to the companies move to its current location in Urbana.

The Neil Street Location of Frasca Aviation. The company moved to its current location in 1990.

Paul Poberezny (Founder of EAA) and Rudy
at Frasca Field

With daughters Peggy and Liz in the Wildcat.

Rudy as a cartoon!

Accepting recognition for Iraq simulators.

Receiving UAA Award

View from the cockpit.

Yes, cars too!

Grandpa said I can solo the Spitfire on my first birthday. So many endorsements, so little time...

Rudy's youngest Grandchild, Joseph.

Rudy & Lucille with their children, in-laws and grandchildren employed at Frasca International.

In Alaska with Lucille

Early Frasca family trip in the Cessna 310

The SNJ and Fiat in formation.

At Glenview National Station. The beginning of his career in flight training.

Rudy and Hal Shevers, founder of Sporty's at Oshkosh 2011.

Rudy with son Bob and grandson Jacob.

The P-40, Spitfire & FOCKE-WULF 190 (FW190) in formation.

The Wildcat in new paint. Flown by David Frasca

Rudy in the SNJ

Rudy and Lucille with Paul and Audrey Poberezny.

From the filming of "1941" in Rudy's P-40

The Frasca Family Circa 1982

Rudy circa 1955

A birds-eye view of Frasca Field

Bob Hoover & Rudy at an airshow

The MK18 Spitfire-up close and personal

Rudy and Lucille

Rudy's Stearman

The Tuskeegee Airmen Reunion in Rantoul, IL with Rudy's P40

The Spitfire and crew at Willard

Professor Tom Page with Rudy as a member of the Illinois Glider Club.

The Frasca family with their Gullwing Stinson circa mid 1970's.

The Frasca family with the Wildcat circa 1973.

Rudy with his beloved Piper Cub.

Rudy flying the Wildcat over Central Illinois

Rudy and Pappy Boyington. Pappy was the inspiration for the TV series "Baa, Baa Black Sheep."

Talk show host Mike Douglas at the Controls of an early Frasca simulator.

The Chipmunk

The Fairchild PT23

Rudy with an early Link simulator at the University of Illinois

Rudy walks the factory floor at the Neil Street location.

Some of Frasca's more recent products.

A gorgeous view of Rudy's MK18 Spitfire in flight.

David Frasca, Bob Hoover, Matt Nightingale, Tom Frasca and Barron Hilton with the FW190
at the Reno Air Races, 2010

Aerial view of Frasca Field

The Frasca Bus- used both for traveling to trade shows and family vacations!

Frasca family circa 1982 on Rudy's 50th Birthday.

Rudy & Lucille with eight well behaved children.

Rudy's Airplane Rides...always a hit!

Rudy & Son John with a Frasca flight simulator.

Rudy flying the Mentor™ at UAA, 2011.

In the Navy...Rudy backrow, second from the left.

Photos taken while filming "The Battle of Midway" The movie featured Rudy's FM-2 Wildcat.

Rudy Frasca, right, president of Champaign's Frasca Aviation, Inc. is greeted by U.S. Ambassador to France Sargent Shriver (center), and the Ambassador's associate director (left) at a reception for U.S. aviation industry exhibitors at the Paris Air Show earlier this month.

Tom, Joe and Rudy Frasca after an airshow.

The P-40 at sunset

Rudy flies the Great Lakes

The P-40 in flight

Rudy with George and Barbara Bush at the Palm Springs Air Museum Benefit. (1988)

Aviation Friends and Memories:

CHAPTER 28

The Passing of Time

Over the years, we have made a lot of friends in aviation, some of whom are getting quite up in age. As time goes by, we become more and more concerned about losing them. One such friend is Elmer Ward.

I've known Elmer for years and appreciate his friendship as well as his active support of warbird preservation. During his 73 years he has owned and restored numerous P-51 Mustangs, an F8F Bearcat painted in Gulf Hawk colors, and a beautifully restored Sea Fury. Elmer has always done a first class job on all his restorations as witnessed by the significant attention they receive from the crowds on the Oshkosh ramp every year.

At Oshkosh, in 1993, both Elmer and I participated in a warbird fly-by. We all lined up and taxied slowly toward the end of the runway for takeoff. Elmer was about number eight in line, followed by Bill Dodds in his P-40, Jeff Ethyl, who was in my Mark 18 Spitfire, and then me in my P-40. As Elmer rolled down the runway on takeoff Bill Dodds taxied into position but didn't start his takeoff roll as soon as normal. He hesitated for a bit, then pushed the throttle forward, and the P-40 roared down the runway and lifted off. Later, Bill said he felt Elmer hadn't been accelerating as rapidly as he should have and he wanted to give him plenty of room if there were a problem; it turned out he had a real problem.

Elmer got off the ground but immediately began losing power

until the engine quit. At that point he was off-airport at a low altitude. With no options available, Elmer crashed into a watery grass area just off the airport causing his wings and engine to separate from the airplane. Bill was flying overhead and began circling the area as the aircraft impacted the ground. He alerted the tower over the radio and, in a gesture to let Elmer know help was on the way, continued to circle the crash site until they got Elmer out of the aircraft. While the aircraft was totally destroyed, the ground team announced that Elmer had been pulled out and would be transported to the local hospital. Dodds then joined up with us, and we did our fly-bys.

Although we worried about Elmer during his hospital stay, in the end he came out just fine. A few months later, at a warbird meeting in Texas, I told Elmer how happy I was to see him in good shape. He just smiled and shrugged his shoulders as if to say "these things happen." Then, without a second thought on the subject, he went on to tell me how he was preparing to bring his P-51 to France for a reenactment of the Normandy invasion. And upon his return from France, he was planning to rebuild his F-8 Bearcat! It was obvious that being 73 and surviving a serious airplane accident wasn't slowing him down a bit.

Unfortunately, time eventually takes us all and we lost our dear friend Delbert Koener. Born in 1902, Delbert had learned to fly in the early '20s. His pilot certificate bore the signature of Orville Wright. In 1927, Delbert started Koener Airport in Kankakee, IL. which still exists in the same location. In 1938, his main hanger destroyed by a storm, he immediately set about to single-handedly design and build a new one. His excellent engineering and construction skills are typified by the fact that the hanger is still in regular use today. During WWII Delbert flew P-40's and even had quite a bit of time in the OX-5.

Over the years Delbert maintained the airport faithfully accentuating the early days of flying. I enjoy just flying to his airport and looking around, and always make a point of taking one of our older aircraft for the trip. Koener Airport rents tail wheel aircraft reminiscent of days-gone-by such as a J-3 Cub, PT-17 Stearman and a Piper Pacer. Four generations of Koeners have helped operate the airport.

Delbert's funeral was like a "Gathering of Eagles." Old friends that I hadn't seen in years were in attendance. As my son Joe did an aerobatic routine in the P-40 to honor Delbert, I reminisced with former FBO owners, airline pilots, and other long-time aviation professionals who were now all in their 80's. These were the people that I had known when I was first getting started in aviation back in the 1940's. They were the ones who were my instructors, ran the FBOs I frequented, and flew for the airlines and corporations back then. They had come from all over the country to pay tribute to a pioneer in Illinois aviation. Everyone agreed that Delbert had done a wonderful job of maintaining the historic 1930's style of aviation. The family plans to carry on Delbert's tradition at Koener Airport, so we expect to be frequent visitors for many years to come. They plan to visit Frasca Field during our fly-ins .

CHAPTER 29

Old Friends

I ran into Rick Seigfreid, the son of an old friend, one pleasant spring morning at the Morris airport about 90 miles north of Champaign. He had just arrived in an AT-6 that he co-owned with two other people. Rick's the spitting image of his dad and my old flying buddy, Bob Seigfreid. Bob and I started flying together when we were 18 years old and just out of high school. I had joined the Navy by then and was based at Glenview Naval Air Station north of Chicago. On weekends, and whenever else we could manage, we would go out to Elmhurst Airport, about ten miles southwest of where O'Hare International Airport is located, and fly a Piper PA-11 together.

The PA-11 was based on the Piper J-3 Cub and had a 65 horsepower engine that was shrouded with a cowling rather than having its cylinders sticking out in the open air. Its two seats were in tandem, front and back, and the pilot sat in the front seat. Another feature of the aircraft was it had heel brakes alongside the rudder pedals rather than the rudder pedal/toe brake combination found in later aircraft.

In those days, Bob and I were a bit more adventurous, so we couldn't simply go out and fly. We were forever having some sort of competition with one another. One of our favorites was to see who could land the little airplane in the shortest distance. We'd take turns landing to see who had brought the aircraft to a full stop using the least runway. One day, in an over-zealous effort to stop in the short-est distance ever, Bob managed to put his heels right through the floorboard of the aircraft! It was an expensive victory, to say the least.

Bob Seigfreid, another friend, Bob Boss, and I continued to fre-quent Woodale Airport but with more of an eye toward the future. Both Bobs pursued the airlines in an industry that is characterized by cyclical boom and bust. They hit it just right and ended up retiring as United Captains after long, rewarding careers. Rick, one of Bob Seigfried's boys, followed in this father's footsteps and also pursued an airline career - becoming a United Captain and war bird enthusi-ast. Despite my love of flying, my experiences in the Navy as a flight simulator instructor resulted in my becoming very dedicated to the concept of simulation. So, after the war, Seigfreid and Boss took up flying careers. I chose to go to the University of Illinois to study and to work in the Aviation Psychology Department specializing in flight simulation studies. (My goal was to manufacture flight simulators).

Talking with Rick that Spring morning, I thought I'd tell him a story about how wild his dad had been as a youth. I related how his father had once had a flat tail wheel in a BT-13 WWII Trainer, but he didn't let it stop him. He held the brakes, gave that 450 horsepower engine more power, pushed the stick forward, and the tail simply came off the ground by itself. Unfettered by the flat tail wheel, Bob rode the brakes, taxied out, and took off without ever letting the tail back down on the ground.

Rick chuckled and told me he was very familiar with that incident. He and his father were going to fly a Twin Beech one day when they discovered their tail wheel was flat. The Twin Beech had been a WWII multiengine trainer which also used the 450 horsepower engine, two of them in fact, which was a lot of power for that airplane. Rick was prepared to look for a local mechanic to fix the Twin Beech's flat but his dad simply smiled and, while relating his BT-13 incident, he increased power on both engines, pushed the wheel forward, taxied out, and took off with the tail wheel raised the entire time!

Bill was another friend I used to fly with, even as far back as when we attended Proviso East High School in Maywood, Illinois from 1945 to 1949. If it can be said that one matures and settles with age, those days were clearly long before settling occurred. One day we took off from Sky Haven Airport in two Piper Cubs with the intention of flying over our high school football field. After making a low pass over the football field (where I should have been practicing), I turned back toward Sky Haven to land. Bill, on the other hand, decided to fly over the Northwestern University football game. Looking off his wingtip he saw a Navion aircraft in a police paint scheme! The policeman followed Bill back to the airport where he immediately grounded him for flying too low over the game. Bill argued that he was legal the whole time and eventually took the issue to court where he won, but the ordeal took a long time and was very expensive in legal fees. That flying policeman should have seen Bill earlier.

Bill was always "pushing the outside of the envelope" as we used to say. I remember one time I was sitting outside at Sky Haven Airport looking to the north, day-dreaming, when I saw a Piper J-5 approaching. The 75 h.p. J-5 had a seat for the pilot in front and a two-passenger seat in the back. After a minute or two the airplane suddenly inverted and did a split S maneuver which struck me as somewhat odd for that aircraft. To my surprise, after it landed, out stepped Bill and he began trying to extricate his very upset girlfriend from the back seat. Bill had attempted to do a slow roll in the aircraft but couldn't get it done properly causing it to go into an uncontrolled split S maneuver. He pulled so many "g's" that his girlfriend slid under her seatbelt up to her chest and was having trouble getting untangled. She learned one of the most important lessons about Bill. You never knew what to expect. I was always pretty tolerant of Bill's whimsy, but one day even I drew the line.

Bill and I were out flying a J-3 Cub with the side open. Bill was sitting up front admiring the view and trying to take pictures; I was flying from the aft seat. He kept moving around, trying to get into just the right position to take pictures, which was somewhat amusing considering the entire side of the airplane next to his seat was wide open. I watched him shift, reposition and squirm until I thought he was going to fall out of the airplane. Suddenly he released his seat belt, turned and handed me his camera and shouted "Give it to me when I reach for it." I said "What do you mean when you reach for it?" And he told me he was going to crawl out of the airplane onto the strut. I was stunned and said: "You are not!" I shouted almost hysterically. "You get back in and put on your seatbelt!" I then rolled the airplane in the opposite direction and started a rapid descent back to the airport after he buckled in.

I always get the biggest kick out of talking to my old friends about flying in the old days and talking to their kids is almost as much fun. But after talking with Bob Seigfreid's son Rick, I realized that all the enthusiasm and fun we had back in those days isn't limited to us old timers. There's another new generation of pilots evolving that shares the same enthusiasm we had. Sadly, the opportunities for just pure fun flying are much more limited. I admit being a bit careless in the old days and do preach safety today. Don't do as I did, I am looking to be around longer.

CHAPTER 30

An Airplane Is One Thing; Encyclopedias Are A Totally Different Matter

During the Summer of 1975, a friend mentioned to me that a WW II German Junkers JU-52 had been flown up from Central America and was being based about 100 miles north of Champaign at Dixon Airport. I had never seen a real JU-52 before and, after a few days of thinking about it, my curiosity got the best of me. I loaded some of the kids into our Mooney aircraft, and we flew up to Dixon one sunny, weekend day. The Junkers was really a sight to behold: a real-life piece of history. It is a three-engine fixed landing gear transport. After looking her over really good, the kids and I began to stroll around the airport and look in the open hangars.

As is the case with many pilots when visiting a new airport, I always enjoy looking at people's airplanes. As we looked into a community hangar, I spotted a Stinson Gullwing all the way in the back, so we went inside to take a closer look. To my surprise, she turned out to be an original Gullwing! She had the fuselage of a straight wing Stinson, the 1937 SR6B model, but with a Gullwing and a 245 horsepower engine. It was now an SR7B. And to make it even better, she was beautifully restored. Like a moth to a flame, I found myself moving toward the office of Gordy Rutt, airport manager and the restorer of the Gullwing. I struck up a conversation with him about the weather, the airport, and flying in general then casually said, "Nice Gullwing, is she for sale?" "Uh huh," he replied even more casually, like a poker player holding a flush in a high stakes game. We chatted some more about the weather, the airport, and flying in general; then even more casually I asked, "How much?" "$10,000," he said matter-of-factly.

My mind began to run through a short list of the airplanes I already owned as the kids looked at me with that "Oh, oh, Dad's gonna buy another airplane" look. I would have taken her on the spot, but I just didn't know how Lucille would react to yet another airplane; she was still kind of miffed about some encyclopedias I had bought on the spur of the moment a month before. Finally, the husband gene in me overcame the awestruck little boy gene. I smiled and said, "That airplane will make some lucky pilot really happy," and we headed back to the Mooney for the trip home. But my mind kept seeing that beautifully restored Gullwing all the way home and for days afterwards.

About a week or so after the trip to Dixon, I happened to be talking with another airplane enthusiast and mentioned the Gullwing. I told him how nicely it had been restored, what it looked like, and everything I could remember about it. After several minutes of listening to me going on and on about it, he smiled and asked, "You trying to convince me it's a good deal or yourself?" Well, I confessed and told him I'd been thinking about buying it but wasn't sure how I'd approach Lucille about getting another airplane. His response was, "Don't tell her!" He then explained his comment. He said if a husband discusses the possibility of buying an airplane with his wife to try to get her consent, the odds are he'll never end up buying the airplane. "There'll always be a hundred reasons why not to buy an airplane," he said. "Just go out and buy it. She'll find out about it in a couple of weeks." He undoubtedly saw a healthy amount of skepticism on my face, so he continued. "Look," he said patiently, almost fatherly, " you'll argue; she'll be angry for a couple hours. Hey, you may lose a wife, but you'll have an airplane!" he laughed. Then in a very reassuring tone he added, "The odds are she'll accept the situation, reluctantly, and that'll be that."

So, armed with my recently acquired outlook on purchasing aircraft, I loaded up the kids in the Mooney again and flew back to Dixon. The Stinson was still in the hangar and still unsold, but some time had passed, and I decided I would do a little dickering. I strolled into Gordy's office prepared to do some good, old-fashioned horse trading. This time I was direct and to-the-point, figuring he'd open up with $10,000 again and I'd counter with maybe $7,000. "So, Gordy, I see the Stinson is still sitting in the hangar. What'll you sell her for?" I asked. "$6,000," he replied. "Sold!" I almost shouted, and the kids all rolled their eyes and wondered if they'd have a home to return to. A few days later a friend flew me to Dixon airport where I concluded the purchase with Gordy, and he gave me a check ride. I then flew the airplane to University of Illinois - Willard Airport where I had arranged to have it hangared. Now I had a real problem because I still hadn't told Lucille.

As the week went by, my anxiety level kept growing. By Sunday morning I was practically a mental case. Since it was a beautiful day, I suggested to Lucille that we go for an airplane ride after church. On the way to the airport I couldn't keep quiet anymore. "Lucille, I've sinned. I bought an airplane!" I stammered. "I know," she said. "Somebody told me about it when you bought it. You know, Rudy, when I married you, I knew you were an aero nut. There's not much I can do about it, so I just accept it. I think it's great, but you shouldn't have gone out and bought those encyclopedias last month, we already have a set!"

Well, that was like a license to steal in my mind. I sent the encyclopedias back, got a refund, and have since bought, sold and collected airplanes without guilt. But I learned my lesson, too. I never buy anything for the house without discussing it with Lucille first.

CHAPTER 31

The Great Jungle Gym Site Debate

Those of my friends who are not in aviation have a funny idea of what a life in the business must be like. Seeing that, in addition to a successful simulation business, we own an airport and fixed base operation, they make certain assumptions. I am frequently told how nice it must be to have the autonomy to do anything I wish. I'll readily admit that owning Frasca Field gives me some business travel flexibility, and even a fair amount of enjoyment, but autonomy? Not hardly. That particular "observation" tends to come more from individuals who have never been married.

Owning Frasca Field has its advantages and disadvantages. Lucille, myself, all of our children, plus their wives, husbands and children, are all involved in aviation in one way or another. One significant advantage of owning our own airport is that it serves as a focal point for the whole family.

We built Lucille's Flying School and Hot Dog Stand on Frasca Field specifically to be a gathering place for customers, friends and family. Situated next to our grass runway, it is built onto an existing hangar and designed to be reminiscent of the early, barnstorming days of flying. The nostalgic, comfortable atmosphere makes an ideal setting to sit on the front porch, have cookouts, and watch airplanes take off and land, and fly our own aircraft literally from the doorstep. On the other hand, a major disadvantage of Frasca Field is that it serves as a focal point for the whole family! Take, for instance, the great Jungle Gym debate.

Apparently, the topic of adding a Jungle Gym to the airport had been discussed by family members for some time prior to my becoming aware of it. For those who have never had grandchildren, or have otherwise managed to blissfully elude knowledge of Jungle Gyms and other such devices, it is a piece of children's recreational equipment. Actually, a better description would be: A knot of steel tubing upon which grandchildren may climb, hang, twist and otherwise intentionally put themselves into harm's way.

Kids love Jungle Gyms because they can hang upside down until all the blood rushes to their head and their eyes bug out; apparently a very cool thing for kids to do. Parents love it because it keeps all the kids riveted in a single location allowing mom and dad to easily maintain a watchful eye while otherwise participating in the festivities of the day. Grandparents, I would later discover, really love it because they can spend the day with the grandchildren and take a nap at the same time. In fact, it appears everyone loves a Jungle Gym, with the possible exception of insurance agents.

This is where that autonomy myth rears its ugly head. The previously mentioned family discussion, I was told, centered on the increasing number of grandchildren coupled with an increasing amount of time their respective families were spending at the airport. Being the patriarch of the clan, THE Frasca upon whose name the word Field is appended, the family unanimously agreed that I should be told a Jungle Gym would be erected. Son-in-law Gene Johnson agreed to undertake the duty of erecting it and then, almost as an afterthought, asked "where do you want me to put it?"

The question of exactly where to locate the Jungle Gym hadn't occurred to me up to that point. I looked around and casually pointed to a spot slightly off to one side of the hangar, out of the way of the front porch. For all the controversy that suggestion caused, you'd have thought I had recommended putting the thing in California! First to object were my daughters. They said it would be impossible for them to sit inside, or even on the front porch, and watch the children at the same time as the location in question would be out of view. I pointed out that Lucille's Flying School and Hot Dog Stand had been built where it was because it provided a wonderful view of the grass runway, allowing me to sit on the porch and watch airplanes take off and land. I didn't think it unreasonable to not want that view blocked by a piece of playground equipment. I glanced at Gene for support and found he had become preoccupied looking at the grass. So I looked up at Lucille, my life companion, for moral support and was instantly met with her disapproving look. She didn't have to say a single word, it was in her eyes. "You think we should put the Jungle Gym right there, huh?" I said, pointing to a spot falling directly between my favorite place to sit and the grass runway. Lucille smiled the smile she gets when she feels I have seen the light.

Now if you think that is the way it really happened, as the old cliché goes, I've got a bridge I'd like to sell you. That is how Lucille remembers it but the truth is, I didn't give in that easily. You see, even though I named the facility Lucille's Flying School and Hot Dog Stand, it was just a coincidence that my wife's name is also Lucille. She wanted to sue me for using her name, but I finally convinced her that it was merely a coincidence. After all, it was built to be a pilot's club house.

The club house is my turf. Lucille has her turf, the house, and I have mine, the club house. The club house is a macho thing, for male pilots. It's a place where guys can have secret meetings, fly airplanes, hangar fly, tell jokes, and have a few beers after flying. You know, no girls allowed. Well the club house became pretty popular and some of my pilot friends began having fly-ins. That's where the trouble began.

Some of the guys who came to our fly-ins started bringing their girlfriends and wives; some even brought children! Our family started scheduling birthday parties there and before long departments in our company started scheduling lunch meetings. We had Christmas parties with Santa Claus flying in with Mrs. Claus and more children. We even had a bunny rabbit parachute in during a company Easter party. It got to be so well known that customers asked to use it for their teenage children's birthday parties so they could give airplane rides. Before I even knew what was happening, the United Way proposed an annual kickoff, of course, in the club house, which included an air show. After the United Way, there were more service groups asking to use it for lunch meetings, to also include a tour of the museum. One year, our kids scheduled a birthday party for Lucille; the entertainment included a nearby tornado! There was even an all-girl lunch from the company; all girls! On weekends, my privacy was invaded by my children bringing my grandchildren. What was happening here? Enter the idea of a Jungle Gym. My own children wanted to set it up on Grandpa's turf. You can well understand my anxiety; I was beginning to lose hold.

My son-in-law Gene did agree to take on the set-up responsibilities, no doubt pressed into service by my daughters, and was aided by a contingent of male family members; not too difficult to guess who volunteered them either. Being the good guy that I am, I agreed to the Jungle Gym and I told them where it should be set up. Any fair-minded person would agree that it should be off to one side so as not to block the view, from the front porch, of aircraft landing and taking off on the sod runway. When my daughters told me that was not an acceptable location, that they preferred to put it directly in front of the building, and directly blocking my view, I disagreed. I did finally agree to another location, one I felt was very acceptable, which would not block the view of the runway from the front porch. That is when I began to see who ran things in the family, including my club house!

My daughters complained to Lucille. Lucille and I discussed the issue when she came out to the airport fighting mad. I showed her the location, the perfect location mind you, at which time she told me, her life-mate, that I was the most selfish man on Earth! When she said that, just for a second, it flashed through my mind that if she would put that on a plaque, I would hang it on my office wall. I failed to mention the thought to her, however, as she told me exactly where the Jungle Gym would be placed, turned her back on me, got in the car and drove home. As I watched her drive off and, admittedly when she was out of earshot, I yelled out that I would move the club house 50 feet!

I then pulled the J-3 Cub out of the hangar, went into the club house, and got a roll of toilet paper. I definitely needed to vent some steam, so I stormed back out to the airplane, propped it myself, climbed into the cockpit, and with the side wide open, took off clutching the toilet paper. At 2,000 feet, I flipped the toilet paper out the door so that it would unroll and stream downward. I then proceeded to dive at the toilet paper and cut it in half. I repeated the cutting passes three more times, decimating that roll of toilet paper. I then landed, taxied back to the ramp, shut the engine off and put the airplane away. I felt better. Maybe I should move my rocking chair over 15 feet.

CHAPTER 32

A Par 8 Takeoff

Everyone has a few skeletons in their closet, and I'm no exception. One of my partners, Clyde (Sonny) Bennish, and I flew to Lake Geneva, Wisconsin for the day in our 1946-65 horsepower Luscombe. Unfortunately, there wasn't an airport near the part of town we wanted to visit, but we did notice a nice golf course. Sonny looked over at me with one of "those looks", and I immediately knew what he was thinking. "Well, let's go!" we simultaneously shouted above the noise of the engine. So, I shrugged my shoulders and set her up on a short final for a nice, straight fairway with nobody in sight. We glided over some trees, touched down softly on the almost manicured sod, and taxied under some trees near the road.

Just as we were getting out of the airplane a police car pulled up along a side road. As the policeman walked in our direction, Sonny scurried around the airplane and opened up the cowling. With his head buried inside and looking real busy, I became the target for the policeman. He asked if we had a problem, and I said the first thing that came into my mind, "Yes, we had a forced landing. It turns out my partner accidentally turned off the gas lever with his foot."

The policeman stood there for a few seconds looking first at me, then at Sonny who was peering around the cowling access door, then back at me. "You're pretty sure about that?" asked the policeman with a healthy amount of skepticism in his voice. He obviously didn't believe us but what could he do? "You two going into town then?" he asked. "Yes" I replied, "would you mind dropping us off?" As we were riding in with him he turned to Sonny and said, "You're sure you had a forced landing?" Well, what could he say at that point? "Yes, officer, it was a foolish mistake but everything's alright now," I interrupted. As we got out of the car and began walking away, he kept watching us until we turned a corner. He was not a happy policeman.

After we did some sightseeing around Lake Geneva and had lunch, we worked our way back to the golf course. Looking down our fairway, which had a row of trees along the right edge, I realized that it was a par 3. I calculated this particular Luscombe, with its tired 65 horsepower engine, had about a par 6 takeoff capability. To make matters worse, the airplane had a fixed pitch, cruise prop which is efficient at cruise but not so hot on takeoff. It seemed that we were in somewhat of a dilemma. Sonny started looking around for one of the greens to see which way the flag was flapping so we'd know the wind when he realized that there were actually two fairways pretty well aligned with each other. Presto! We suddenly had a par 8 runway with the wind coming straight down it toward us!

After moving some benches out of the way, we fired her up and taxied to the far, downwind end of the fairway. There was a golfer just walking up to the tee as we arrived. Taking one long, astounded look at us, he just signaled for us to play through. So I checked the mags, gave her power, and we began bumping our way down the fairway, kicking up loose divots as we went.

Well, the two of us in that little airplane with a tired engine plodded down the grass for a lot longer than either one of us were expecting. It was a good thing we had the second fairway on the opposite end, but it didn't take long before we were beginning to get uncomfortably close to the end of that one too. A smokestack and a large tree began to figure prominently at the end of the second fairway. About that time the Luscombe lightened up, and I gently coaxed her off the sod and into the air. We had enough speed to enter a fairly steep bank to maneuver between the tree and smokestack, then kept on coming around until we were flying low over the fairway in the direction from which we had just come. As we approached the golfer who was just about to tee off, I yelled "FORE!" out the window. I then banked right toward home as the golfer probably sliced into the woods. It was one of the dumbest things I have done!

When Hollywood Calls...
Or my career as a Movie Star

CHAPTER 33

Filming The Movie "Midway"

One of the aspects of my career in aviation that I most enjoy is the diversity. I feel very fortunate to be able to participate in so many different activities that center around flying. This includes the simulation business, flight school, FBO, museum, flying the warbirds, doing air shows, and watching my entire family participate in these things together. Certainly one of the most unusual and most interesting of all has been my participation in the making of feature films. It all started in 1980 when I received a call from Frank Pine of the TallMantz Museum on the Orange County Airport in Southern California.

The museum was a partnership between Pine and Frank Tallman, an old Navy friend from my Glenview Naval Air Station days. Tallman had been a WWII pilot who stayed on with the reserves after the war and was assigned to Glenview NAS. His burning interest in antique aircraft and especially WWII warbirds caused him to slowly build up a sizable, personal collection of aircraft. Eventually, he migrated to California with all his aircraft and teamed up with well-known Hollywood pilot Paul Mantz. Over the years, their combined effort through the TallMantz Museum resulted in a solid reputation with the movie industry for supplying authentic, vintage aircraft and superior pilots for many feature films.

Pine had called me to say that a feature film was being developed about the battle of Midway and they needed two Wildcats for the flying scenes. He told me he had already made an agreement with Junior Burchnell down in Texas for the use of his aircraft and wanted to know if I would be interested in letting them use my Wildcat as the second aircraft. Well, I've always been a WWII history buff, and I knew Junior's reputation as a very colorful figure with a large collection of his own aircraft, so it sounded like too much fun to pass up. Pine and I quickly settled on $150.00 per flying hour for the Wildcat, $100 per day for me, plus expenses, which is what I was charging back in those days.

I flew the aircraft down to Whiting Field in Pensacola, Florida about a week early to make sure it would be there on time. The plan was to shoot the scenes on board a real aircraft carrier out on an actual cruise. It obviously wouldn't do to be delayed by bad weather enroute and miss the carrier's departure. Nobody actually intended to take off and land those old warbirds on the carrier; they would be loaded and off-loaded by crane. After I arranged for temporary storage in a hangar at Whiting Field, I looked up an old friend, Bob Blaky. Bob was involved with the Naval Air Museum at Pensacola, and I spent some time visiting with him and looking around the museum. Eventually, I took an airline back home to wait for the carrier's departure date a week later.

The day finally arrived to begin the cruise, and I showed up bright and early to board the U.S.S. Lexington. The Lexington was in use during WWII and was still being used to carrier qualify Naval pilots. In fact, we were going along with the Lexington on a training cruise. Departure from Pensacola was scheduled for Monday at 0800 hours to Corpus Christi with a scheduled return time of 1700 hours on the following Friday. The plan was to shoot the deck and hangar scenes for the movie in between actual Naval training missions.

We towed our aircraft out to the ship with the wings folded so they could be hoisted on-board the carrier. Once on deck, they were moved to the carrier's elevator and sent down to the lower deck where they were securely fastened for the voyage. As I watched the very efficient and organized crew move even these old WWII aircraft, I couldn't help but think back to my own Naval career.

I was in the Navy from 1949 to 1952. I joined at age 18, right out of high school, with the hope of becoming a pilot. I applied to be a Naval Flight Cadet, but because I lacked two years of college, my application was turned down. As it turned out, it was one of the best things that could have happened to me. I ended up becoming a Link Trainer instructor teaching pilot cadets, a job that would eventually lead to my life-long involvement with flight simulation. Because of my assignment, I never set foot on-board a ship even though I spent three years in the Navy. Now, watching them load my airplane, I couldn't help but chuckle with the realization I was not only about to embark on a Naval cruise but it would be with my own historic fighter on-board a historic aircraft carrier!

We weren't on-board very long before a briefing was called of all the movie personnel. I was introduced to two actors who would be "flying" the Wildcats, Eric Estrada and Eddie Albert Jr., and we struck up a close relationship. As we listened to the briefing, I kept looking at Estrada and Albert in their WWII flight uniforms and was struck by how much they looked the part. At one point Albert turned to me and asked what it was like to be in that aircraft with the cockpit on fire. The question sort of took me by surprise, and I laughed and said I had no idea since it had never happened to me. It did make me wonder why he asked that question!

Eventually we were assigned sleeping compartments, and I went down to stow my gear and inspect the small space. That night, as I lay on one of the two bunks, I looked up at the ceiling and wondered about the pilots that slept on this bed during the war. The motion of the ship, combined with the long day's excitement, proved to be better than any sleeping pill ever made. But morning came quickly, and I woke up hungry and ready to meet the day.

First stop was the Officer's Mess for a hearty breakfast. By the time I arrived Charlton Heston, Glenn Ford and most of the actors were already eating. I introduced myself and sat down, planning on a nice, leisurely breakfast chatting with some very famous people. As I was taking my first sip of coffee the director, Jack White, entered the Mess. I asked him about our first day's schedule, and he looked me right in the eye and said, "As we speak, your airplane is being prepared to go up the elevator!" He didn't have to add "and why aren't you with it?". So much for chatting with the stars. I quickly dashed out of the Mess and down the stairwell to the lower deck, arriving at the elevator just ahead of the Wildcat.

Standing next to my own Wildcat as it was being elevated to, and moved on, the carrier's huge flight deck was quite an experience. There I was, looking out over the deck, seeing that big Island off to one side with a giant number 16 painted alongside the smokestack. I observed the crew as they moved the two Wildcats into position and secured them to the deck. I kept shooting everything that happened with my 8mm movie camera.

I don't remember how much film I had brought with me, but it wasn't enough; I ran out that first morning. Fortunately, there was a PX on board that sold 8mm film; I was their best customer for the entire cruise! I was constantly taking movies of everything that happened. Everyone kept joking about how I was shooting more film than the movie crew. There is one shot in particular where Junior and I start up our Wildcats on deck. It shows the engines starting, the puffs of smoke from the exhaust stacks, the Navy flight deck crew, dressed in their various colored shirts, holding fire bottles and performing various tasks. In the end I got the last laugh because I had some terrific shots, and by the time it was all over the other guys wished they had done the same.

Most of the scenes were shot with a camera right on the deck of the carrier that was pointed at the two Wildcats. Another camera was located on the carrier's Island for a different perspective. The way they had the cameras set up you couldn't tell both airplanes were actually tied to the ship's deck. After Junior and I started the engines and warmed them up, we jumped out and Estrada and Albert climbed in for the close-up shots. Once back on the deck I pulled out my own camera again and began shooting more footage amid much teasing and joking. All of this was compounded by the fact that we were shooting these scenes in between real jet carrier qualification takeoffs and landings.

One of the truly unique scenes in the movie was the duplication of a real F-6 Hellcat fighter crash on the deck of the carrier that occurred during a later battle. The F-6 had landed on the deck but missed the arresting cable and slid into the Island. The tail section was separated from the cockpit, and the pilot was able to climb out; but the whole incident had been filmed by the carrier's on-board camera. It was rare historic footage that the director wanted to include in the film.

To duplicate the shot, they took Junior's aircraft and moved it up against the Island in the same position as the crashed aircraft had been. They took a bent P-38 propeller and installed it on the Wildcat, unbolted the right landing gear so the aircraft would assume the same angle as the real aircraft that crashed, then set up the camera so it only showed the cockpit forward. The special effects team then set the whole thing up so it looked like there was a real crash and fire. Once everything was ready, Albert got in the cockpit and they shot the scene. It shows him attempting to put out a fire with a fire bottle while airborne, then landing, crashing into the island, passing out, and the flight deck crew running up to him and pulling him out of the airplane. He was made up to look like he had been burned, and I was surprised how well he could portray being unconscious and remaining limp as the crew literally lifted him up and pulled him out of the burning cockpit. While all this was going on a real Naval fire/rescue team was standing very close by in case something went wrong. They had to shoot the same scene several times, and each time Albert would climb back in the aircraft and start all over again. With all the special effects, the large film crew, ship crew and rolling and pitching of the carrier, it was not an insignificant accomplishment.

I remember during the filming of that scene one of the ship's fire/rescue crewmen who was helping out with the production fell on his back, hitting his head rather hard. Charlton Heston rushed over to his aid; I'll bet that sailor still talks about being rescued by Heston on-board a carrier. Finally the scene was done, and if you watch the film you'd never know that they married up the actual crash footage of the F-6 shot during WWII with the scene we had shot on board the Lexington. It looks as real as if it had been all shot on the day of the actual crash.

A day or so later, they were shooting another scene, and I was standing there on the island deck filming them with my 8mm camera. Suddenly, Jack White looked up from the camera right at me, and he didn't look at all happy. It turned out that when he looked into his camera at the scene, I was in there staring back at him with my own camera! I backed off sheepishly and found something distant to occupy my time with for the rest of that scene, but it wouldn't be the last time my camera and I would take center stage. There was a scene shot in the lower deck hangar in which they simulated an on-board fire. I was amazed at how realistic the special effects people could make that fire, and I just kept shooting it from various angles with my camera. Well, the scene called for Charlton Heston to run across the hangar with the flames in the background, and it was just too realistic for me to miss. So there I am filming the scene as Heston runs across the hangar right into me! "Oh no! Not you again!" was all he could say as he raced by me. I'm afraid I was beginning to get a reputation for being in the wrong place at the wrong time. But talk about being in the wrong place at the wrong time, the day the Russians arrived had to be the funniest incident of the cruise.

One day, when the Wildcats were secured in tie downs on the lower hangar deck, all the Naval aircraft launched on a training exercise. There we were on a WWII aircraft carrier with the only two planes on board being WWII Wildcat fighters. It was like a page out of history. It was that exact moment that the Navy flew in some Russian Admirals for a tour of the carrier. Can you imagine the image of the U.S. Navy they left with?

"All good things must come to an end" as they say, and the week went by very quickly. On the trip home I kept reflecting about what a great week it had been; but I had to chuckle to myself that, as luck would have it, I had tailwinds both going to Pensacola and returning home. That could only happen because I was collecting $150 per flight hour! When I got back to Champaign I made a low pass over the airport and landed. My family and some friends were there wanting to hear all about the week. When the film was finally released, everyone wanted to go and see my airplane in the movies. Just prior to the film's release, the local paper ran an article about my participation, and as a result the local theater called me and invited me to sit through their preview of the film before it opened to the general public. As luck would have it, I was scheduled to leave town the day they planned to do it. I told them I would love to see the preview but was unable to attend that day. The theater manager then offered to give me a private showing of the film and opened up the balcony so my family and I could watch from the best seats in the house. It was a wonderful ending to a great experience.

CHAPTER 34

Filming "1941"

Up to now I had only one experience with Hollywood and it had been very positive. So it was with eager anticipation that I picked up the telephone when my secretary told me I had a call from Hollywood. This time it was someone calling from Universal Studios at the request of director Steven Spielberg.

I was told that Spielberg had been directing a WWII movie comedy called "1941" starring John Belushi. He said there were a few scenes that needed some enhancement; specifically, close up shots of Belushi in a P-40. By chance, Belushi and Dan Aykroyd happened to be in Chicago shooting another film called the "Blues Brothers". Spielberg wondered if I would be willing to fly my P-40 up to Chicago so they could shoot a few scenes for "1941". This would be done in a hangar.

I wasn't very eager to take the aircraft up to Chicago where I wouldn't have much control over it. As an alternative I suggested that Belushi come down to Champaign to shoot the scenes in a University of Illinois hangar. Spielberg agreed and we negotiated a fee of $1000 per day plus expenses for use of the aircraft. In no time at all he had a movie crew in Champaign who began working out the shot set-up.

One of the logistical problems that came up early on was the fact that Champaign did not have airline service at the time because Ozark Airline's pilots were on strike. Spielberg was content to have us pick him up in Chicago in our van and drive him down but Belushi made it very clear he would only fly down. So I arranged with Whatcha McCollum, a local, colorful charter operator to pick Belushi up at Miegs Field in Chicago and return him there when the shooting was completed.

Meanwhile the crew was busy setting up the shot in the hangar at the University of Illinois Willard Airport. We debated about whether the fumes from the fuel in the aircraft would be a problem with all the electrical equipment and lighting and decided it wouldn't. Just to be sure, however, we decided to fill the tanks to minimize the fumes. Then the crew felt, to get the shot to look right, they needed to put the aircraft in flying position; so we jacked up the tail. The P-40 was already painted with water colors with the proper marking for the era. Finally, they set up a huge blue screen behind the aircraft which would provide a neutral background so that in post-production they could project the background behind the aircraft that would make it look as if it were actually in the air. When the movie finally came out it really looked as if it was flying.

Overall, I was surprised with the tremendous amount of time, effort and money that was spent on a scene that turned out to be only about one minute in the movie. In retrospect, looking back on both "Midway" and "1941", I must say I am generally impressed with the technical people I met. They were like a highly skilled and disciplined army. Each person knew exactly what to do, where to go, and when to do it. I was completely fascinated with Spielberg; he was young, already famous with a series of hit movies, and in total control of this large film crew. As it happened, he was also very interested in WWII aircraft. His attention to period detail such as uniforms and the aircraft's paint scheme was amazing.

He asked me if he could sit in the cockpit of my Wildcat – to which I readily agreed. After he climbed into the cockpit, I climbed up to the wing alongside of the cockpit and explained what it was all about.

The day finally came when they were going to shoot the scenes.

Everyone arrived on time, but right from the beginning Belushi was complaining that he was flown down in a propeller-driven airplane. That it was a turboprop (MU-2) didn't seem to matter very much to him. He finally got into the P-40 and they did a rehearsal. Prior to this it was obvious that the P-40 was a mere prop to him as he was rather rough on it a friend told me when they used his P40. So we decided to pad the cockpit as much as possible to protect it. Belushi did a lot of improvising in the scene to see what would work best. As an improvisation he grabbed a fake glass Coke bottle with colored water in it and smashed it over the instrument panel, splashing liquid all over the cockpit. The crew, including Spielberg, most of whom had enormous respect for the aircraft, collectively gasped and looked at me. I guess it would be safe to say that my expression was not one of amusement but I just shrugged it off. At that point everyone laughed and the shot was funny enough that it did get used in the film.

Belushi was always surrounded by a small group of people; they were very protective of him. For instance, I tried to take some pictures during the shooting but they wouldn't let me. Finally we agreed that I could take a few pictures but they would have them developed and send me pictures later; This never happened. His people also kept making remarks about the transportation being a prop plane. They wanted assurance that Belushi would be flown back in a pure jet. So I called Watcha McCollum again and arranged for him to fly them back to Meigs Field in a Learjet which shaved a few minutes off the flight at significant expense. It's no wonder it costs so much to make movies!

In the end, I received $7,000 for the use of the aircraft, part of which I gave to the University of Illinois for the use of their hangar and mechanics. And, of course, I also had the satisfaction of seeing yet another of my aircraft in the movies.

CHAPTER 35

Tora, Tora, Tora

One of the things that has always interested me about the motion picture business is how different everything looks when you see it at the theater. The time and expense the director spends to make the finished film realistic is absolutely astounding. What you see up close during the filming is nothing like the end result. Hollywood can literally make a silk purse out of a sow's ear. Take, for instance, the film "Tora! Tora! Tora!"

The movie, which was about the Japanese attack on Pearl Harbor in 1941, required the use of many different aircraft. Unfortunately, some of the types actually used in the attack were either very scarce or non-existent. One such aircraft was the Japanese Zero fighter. The studio's answer to that problem was to modify old aircraft, which happened to be plentiful, to look like the Zero. Quite a few of them were roughly modified as they were slated to be used only in distant shots. There were, however, quite a few close-up shots that required aircraft with a much higher degree of replication.

Those aircraft that were to be used in close-ups were most commonly modified old AT-6s or SNJs. Their square wing tips were removed and replaced with custom-made round wing tips. The standard 600 hp engines were replaced with geared powerplants that had 3-bladed propellers more closely resembling the original Zero. The rear seat was removed to make the airplane appear to have a single seat cockpit, the tail wheel was made retractable, and an arrester hook was added because that version of the Zero was flown off of aircraft carriers. The finished aircraft closely replicated the original Zero.

If you watch the movie you would swear those were real Zeros but they were simply a really good Hollywood conversion. So good, in fact, that they were not the kind of thing that the producers were willing to mothball and store on some studio back lot. There was a lot of money tied up in those aircraft and it was decided to sell them when filming was complete to partially recover their cost. To those of us interested in warbirds however, the selling price was really fairly inexpensive.

Bill Ross, an old friend of mine, decided he would purchase one of the better Zero replications. He later donated it to the EAA museum. For quite a few years EAA President Paul Poberezny, Gus Limbach (a former WW-II Corsair pilot) or Carol Dietz (an Eastern Air Lines Captain), would fly it in air shows. I can recall a number of occasions over the years, when it was flown by one of the above pilots, when I would "shoot it down" with my Wildcat or P-40. Eventually, the EAA sold the Zero and replaced it with another in better condition.

Sometime later, a Hollywood Zero turned up in Texas and was flown in various air shows. My son, Joe flew it in a few air shows and when it came up for sale we decided to buy it. It was a very accurate replication of a Zero, had been rebuilt, and featured a rebuilt engine. We had been flying it for a while when Bill Ross told me that it was the same aircraft that he had bought and ultimately donated to the EAA museum. It was the same aircraft that Joe and I had been shooting down for years! It now had a different paint job.

This new revelation prompted me to research its history in more detail and I discovered that it was the only aircraft used in the film that actually took off from the U.S. Naval Aircraft Carrier Lexington during filming. It was also the one that was most frequently shot down during the filming for two reasons. First, it featured a smoke system which would produce a trail of smoke behind the airplane after it was "shot down." Movie directors love to see airplanes smoke as they dive "out of control" to a fiery crash. The second reason it was used so extensively in the film is because it had a system whereby two gases were mixed together and ignited to produce machine gun sounds.

We ended up developing a very nice routine with Tom flying the Zero in strafing runs back and forth across the airport in front of the crowd. As he would pass low over the field he would "fire" the machine guns, which was very audible to the crowd. I would run out to the P-40, take off and dogfight with the Zero until Tom would shoot me down. At that point Joe would jump in the Wildcat, engage the Zero and shoot it down. Tom would then fly the Zero off into the distance trailing smoke as Joe proceeded to do a very nice aerobatic routine in the Wildcat. It was always a crowd pleasing Airshow act.

Over the years, Tom flew the Zero in quite a few air shows. He duplicated the old dog fighting act on many occasions and took on everything from T-34s to Corsairs and P-51s. In addition, he worked out an excellent aerobatic routine with it that has been well received by many Airshow enthusiasts. Our Zero has proven to be a very reliable and entertaining aircraft. Not bad for an airplane that started off as a "sow's ear!"

A Hollywood Zero model of our Zero was made by one of Champaign's model aircraft companies. Numerous models of our aircraft followed.

The Family and Business
of Aviation

CHAPTER 36

My Formula For Success

I remember when I was 18 years old I heard on the radio that a very successful businessman had passed away. The announcer quoted the man, who had some years earlier explained how he had become so successful.

The man had said his formula for success could be broken down into three simple steps. First, you want to know what it is that you want to do. Second, you must study and analyze the situation. Third, you must use the initiative to get it done. It sounded very simple and straight forward, so I began facing the challenges of life using those three steps. Since that day, my life has been moving along fairly effectively in the right direction. Of course, you have to define what you mean by success.

Just about anyone you ask will give you a different definition of success. For a while my definition changed frequently because I probably was a bit short-sighted; my goals were too specific and too short ranged. But over the years, I've developed my own definition that has served me well. I believe success is attaining one's goals without stepping on the feet of others. Success, of course, should not be confused with satisfaction. Achieving success does not guarantee happiness, that is something that comes from within, from knowing one has done the best they can do given the circumstances.

Contrary to popular opinion, there's nothing wrong with people who are "never satisfied" with their work; it is that feeling that makes one strive to do better. However, certain periods of contentment should exist or you would live under the pressure to achieve constantly. I have grown to a position where those two opposing forces tend to balance one another, giving me the drive to excel, but allowing me to relax and enjoy that with which I am blessed.

All of this, of course, ties into goals. I read somewhere that only two percent of people have developed a set of goals for themselves. What a very sad situation; life without purpose. When you have a goal, you have a purpose. You can't embark on a journey if you don't have a destination. Having a goal is the first and most fundamental step toward success. Once you have a goal you know what to study; what information to collect for future reference.

I generally don't discriminate about the information I collect; if it pertains to the goal, I collect it. As time goes by the information becomes a part of my collective knowledge as if I had taken a college course in the subject. Occasionally someone will question why I am doing something the way I am and I'm not exactly certain myself. I'll say, "I don't really know, but if you keep questioning me, I'll get the information out and we can both review it."

It is really quite surprising the way things have worked out over the years. Sometimes, I feel that it has all been luck but when I really look back at the decisions I've made, I realize that the collective knowledge I acquired from studying and analyzing, has guided me in my decision making. That, coupled with the initiative to get it done, has been the real reason for whatever success I have had. From the very beginning I set goals and have been moving in their direction ever since.

Not that every decision has been fruitful; some were fairly major mistakes, but the result of every decision produced new information that, when studied and analyzed, became valuable for future decisions. Similarly, there have been times when I would say to myself, "This is just not going to work, I should have gone in a different direction with my life" but somehow I have managed to stick with it regardless. Sometimes the will to continue has come from within and sometimes it has come through the encouragement of Lucille and the children.

Early on, I developed a philosophy which has served me well. Each morning I get up and tell myself, "today is another opportunity to make things work" and you know what? Things have been working very well ever since.

CHAPTER 37

Success and Family

There is no such thing as overnight success. There is no doubt that aviation has provided my family with many opportunities and a good life, but success was achieved after many long, hard years of dedication. The funny thing is that some people seem to think that when one is successful they are suddenly transformed into a different person. Maybe that's true for a movie star but the average business man has both feet planted firmly in reality; that's almost a requirement for success in the first place!

I am frequently asked what kind of plans I have for vacations and holidays by people who expect to hear that I'm taking my entire family to some exotic place. In fact, I am often invited by clients and business associates to vacation in some pretty exotic places. We're fortunate that we do get to see the world quite a bit in our business, but our family is very close and holidays are always spent at home. New Year's day, 1995 is a good example.

That year New Years fell on a Sunday so after church Lucille and I joined some friends for breakfast at a local pancake restaurant. Afterwards, I went to Frasca Field and, with the help of the lineman, pulled my little Piper J-3 Cub out of the museum. It was a very cold, windy, overcast day which reminded me that the last time I flew the Cub there had been a lot of cold air leaking into the cockpit. While the lineman applied preheat to the engine and put some air in the tires, I gathered some shop towels and filled in the most obvious sources of air leaking into the cockpit; not very pretty but expedient. At that point I climbed in the back seat, closed the door and the lineman propped the engine after commenting how cold it was outside. He was shaking his head as he fled from the cold and raced back inside the warm office. I glanced around the airport and noticed that I was the only one out there. I taxied out and took off on Runway 27 because I knew where to go to see other people who love aviation enough to be out on a cold, New Years day. I flew out to the local model airplane field.

It has been a local tradition for years that the radio-controlled model airplane group flies the first day of the year. I circled the model airplane field, which looks like a miniature airport, and the guys started coming out of the building where they had been warming up. During their lull I made a low pass over their little airport, and we waved at one another. They were holding steaming cups of coffee and several of them held up their model airplanes. The details were impossible to see from my vantage point but I've seen enough of them on the ground. They are a true labor of love. Meticulously hand built and painted, they were perfect miniature versions of the real thing.

I was already beginning to feel warmer inside as I turned the Cub westward toward Mahomet. As I flew over the Interstate I realized how windy it really was; the cars below were passing me! I chuckled as I flew over the house my son had just finished building but there were no signs of life, so I proceeded northwest. About 20 miles later I spotted Bob Ashworth's farm and made a low pass over his private airstrip; all was quiet below. I did the same thing at McCully's airstrip north of Champaign and still no sign of life. Then I decided it was time to fly to Dave Mennenga's.

Dave, who was a Frasca employee at the time, and his wife Rita were both aviation enthusiasts and owned a beautifully restored 1939 Piper Cub. They also had three great kids so I knew there would be life in the Mennenga household! I landed on their little airstrip, taxied up to the house and shut down the engine. Rita was in the door waving when I looked up. They invited me in and we had tea and Oreo cookies. I commented that it looked as if I had been the first person to land on his airstrip for the new year. Rita looked at me and asked quizzically, "Why are you flying on a day like this?" She sort of caught me off guard and the only thing that came to mind was, "Rita, this is what I do!" We all laughed but on the flight home I got to thinking about what I'd said. It was New Years day, freezing cold, I could have chosen to be virtually anywhere in the world I wanted, and here I was on my way to a family gathering after ushering in the new year in my little Cub.

I landed back at Frasca Field and taxied up to Lucille's Flying School and Hot Dog Stand. After pushing the Cub back into its hangar I went into the clubhouse to warm up. In a little while the family began arriving for our New Years day gathering. We had lots of food, games and a great, old fashioned family gathering. The clubhouse was alive with everything important in my life: Lucille, my children, the grandchildren, and all the beautiful airplanes in our museum.

After a while I peeked in to check up on the little Cub, like one might check up on a puppy. It was warming up in the hangar, sheltered from the blustery cold, and seemed to smile back at me and say, "This is what success is all about. What better way to spend the New Year than with the family and me?"

CHAPTER 38

Frasca Family Flyers

The Frasca family is truly an aviation family. Every member of the family, from my wife Lucille to my youngest son David, has been integrally involved with the family business. Lucille has spent her life working side-by-side with me, complimenting my strong points and supplementing my weak. It is very clear that the family would not have been successful without her.

Mary, our oldest daughter, kept watch on our campground in Wisconsin for more than one hard winter so we would not have to worry about it during the off season. Eventually she came back to Illinois permanently and became involved in our FBO and now in the accounting department at Frasca. Her husband Gene joined the simulation side of the business and has become a highly reliable and valued team member as our facility manager. Sadly, Gene passed away in June of 2012 after a bout with cancer. He will be greatly missed.

Our son John literally transformed the original Frasca mechanical flight trainer into the computer-driven, state-of-the-art simulator it is today. His guidance and insight into computer-generated simulation not only earned him the title of President, but also transformed Frasca Aviation into Frasca International, a major simulator manufacturer doing business in almost 80 countries.

Two of our daughters, Peg and Liz, learned to fly and have gone on to take active management roles in the simulation business. Peggy handles our advertising and promotions and her husband, Joel is our sales director. Liz has worked in several roles until leaving to start a business with her husband, Graham, who is also a professional pilot.

Somewhere along the way, son Tom fell in love with buying and selling airplanes. His tenacity and creativity have turned up some very interesting aircraft since the days when he purchased his first aircraft, a Luscombe. In addition to selling, Tom also manages our Frasca Air Services Fixed Base operation at the airport and has become a very good pilot in his own right. Bob, who was practically raised in an airplane, is a department manager in our simulation business and flies warbirds with Tom, Dave and old Dad.

David, our youngest, was cause for concern over the years. He didn't seem to have any interest in aviation at all. He was always more interested in hunting, fishing and golf. I recall him asking Lucille one day, "How come Dad doesn't do those things?" We were asking, "Where did we go wrong?" Everyone wondered if he'd been found on the doorstep as an infant. But as he got older, he began to get interested and now holds instrument, commercial and multiengine pilot certificates, flies aerobatics in the T-34 and SNJ, Wildcat and P-40, and has worked on his Aviation Maintenance Technician certificate. He modified a 1940 Piper J-3 and put a 150 hp Lycoming engine on it. He removed the old engine, overhauled it, did some structural work to the aircraft itself, and set it up for aerobatic flying. David worked in our warbird restoration shop at the airport at the time and is now the director of engineering at our flight simulation factory He seems to have found his niche and brings the Frasca family full circle.

CHAPTER 39

Frasca Airport
Two-Day Air Fairs

One of the things I have always enjoyed most about aviation is sharing it with others. For quite a few years our Frasca Air Museum sponsored two-day Air Fairs and fly-ins at Frasca Field. They were very popular. We tried to offer a well-rounded view of the romance and beauty of general aviation.

A very popular part of the fair was the fly-in pancake and sausage breakfast; attracting airplanes and carloads of hungry aviation enthusiasts. After a hearty breakfast folks naturally start strolling through the museum looking at the many static displays. But the real excitement started when we rolled out some of the warbirds and flew them so people could see what those old aircraft really looked like in the air.

With almost everyone in the Frasca family a pilot, we were able to put on our own Airshow routine for the crowd. In addition, there were always friends who would volunteer to do some routines, making the Frasca Air Fair a pretty impressive Airshow by most standards. More importantly, it was always a lot of fun for everyone. Each performance was distinct unto itself but some performances just seem to stand out more clearly in my mind than others. I recall one such time when my son Joe was still alive.

Joe was a pilot's pilot; he just had a feel for the airplane and it showed when he flew. On this particular occasion Joe was in the

Wildcat, I was in the P-40E, and sons Tom and Bobby were in the SNJ and T-34 respectively. We had just made single file fly-bys over the field in front of the crowd when Joe's voice came over the radio. "I'm coming up on your left wing," he said to me, and I saw the Wildcat slide gracefully into position. As we circled around and headed back toward the airport Tom saw us flying in formation and maneuvered the SNJ off my right wing.

There we were, flying in a nice tight formation, and I was thinking Bobby should take up the slot position. As if he could read my mind, Bobby's voice came over the radio and announced he had just maneuvered the T-34 into the slot and, without prior agreement, we had just put together a really beautiful diamond formation and flew in front of an approving crowd. It's one of the real advantages of our flying family; you just sort of get a feeling about what everyone is going to do.

CHAPTER 40

A Real Airport Reliever

All of our kids literally grew up, in and around airplanes. We took them out to the airport and flying with us, even as very small children.

I remember taking Joe out to the University of Illinois airport back in the days when they regularly flew PT-17 Stearmans. The Stearman was a WWII trainer that featured a 220 hp engine; it was very popular for glider towing.

One day I showed up at the airport with three year old Joe just as a friend was getting ready to tow a glider with the Stearman. He looked at the two of us and offered a ride. The Stearman was a biplane with tandem cockpits (one behind the other). I boosted Joe up onto the wing then climbed up after him. I then stepped into the front cockpit, sat down into the seat, put the seat belt and harness on myself, and then lifted Joe into the cockpit and onto my lap. Since there was only a seatbelt and harness for one person, I held him in my arms.

Within a few minutes we were airborne with the glider trailing behind. At about 2,000 feet the glider released from the tow line and, to my complete astonishment, we immediately dove down first doing a split S, then dropped the tow line onto the airport and quickly climbed back to altitude!

He then did a slow roll which left me upside-down, hanging in the seat belt and harness, holding onto Joe with all my strength. Worse, there was no communication capability between cockpits. He went on to do additional aerobatics with me clutching Joe for all I was worth. Finally I was able to attract his attention and he nodded agreement that it was time to land. I was, quite frankly, as shaken by the experience as Joe was enthralled.

The pilot landed the tow plane near the glider which, in those days, was in an area remote from the airport operations area. After our rather wild flight, I definitely had the urge to relieve myself and so did Joe but there was no washroom anywhere near. So I decided it was time to indoctrinated Joe into the way pilot's "do their thing" in the field.

Now in those days, pilots were almost exclusively male, so there was a fairly common practice to handle the situation. They would just go stand alongside the aircraft, on the side opposite everyone, and relieve themselves. Joe got a really big kick out of this and began relieving himself alongside the airplane every chance he got. Later on, back at home, Lucille was horrified when Joe put his new found procedure into practice. He regularly went into the back yard, stood up against the fence, and "did his thing."

CHAPTER 41

Joe Frasca and the U.S. Aerobatic Team

It is difficult to say exactly when Joe decided he wanted to be on the U.S. Aerobatic Team and compete in the international aerobatic arena. What is clear, is that he began to show signs at an early age that he would be a top notch pilot. I had Joe working the controls of an airplane as early as age two-and-a-half; long before most kids learn to ride a bike. While there were many positive benefits from this early exposure, there were some funny ones too.

When we bought Joe his first sled he had a problem figuring out how it worked. He was giving a ride to some friends and they crashed right into a tree. The problem was that Joe had learned how to steer an airplane using his feet on the rudder pedals. With the sled he also had to use his feet to steer but it worked the reverse of the airplane. The first few times he attempted to steer the sled the tracks in the snow showed much "wavering and confusion."

For quite a few years Joe flew regularly and loved it. By the time he was 18 he had flown a variety of light, single engine aircraft and had become a very proficient aerobatic pilot. But by then he was beginning to express a serious interest in moving to larger, more powerful aircraft, especially our Wildcat. I gave it some very serious thought and recalled that during the war that very airplane was flown by young, fresh-out-of-flight school, ensigns. Regardless, I was still concerned that it might be too much airplane for him to handle. Unsure of what to do, I contacted my good friend Paul Poberezny, founder and president of the Experimental Aircraft Association (EAA).

Paul expressed similar concerns then asked what kind of aircraft Joe had been flying up to that point. I told him about the various aircraft but when I included the Cessna 195 Paul almost immediately said Joe shouldn't have any problem at all. With my concerns fairly subsided I called another friend, Bob Ashworth, who had an AT-6 and arranged for Joe to get some dual time in his two-place aircraft as it was a little more like the Wildcat than anything else Joe had flown.

Never one to pass up a good opportunity, I made a deal with Joe. I told him that there were certain conditions I would require before letting him fly the Wildcat. The first was I wanted him to get straight A's that next semester at Southern Illinois University. The second was I wanted him to sell his motorcycle; it always made me very nervous when he rode it. Somewhat to my surprise, Joe immediately agreed unconditionally; we had a deal. And so it was that Joe got checked out in the Wildcat.

It would be an understatement to say it didn't take long for Joe to master the Wildcat. In no time at all he was doing high quality aerobatics. In addition, he became very attached to the airplane and spent quite a bit of time maintaining it, learning it inside and out. After about a year's experience in the Wildcat he began flying it in the Warbird fly-bys at various air shows and soon after was doing an aerobatic routine at Oshkosh.

I recall that first routine at Oshkosh. I was up in the announcer stand watching him take off. He began by lifting off the runway, manually cranking up the gear, holding the airplane close to the ground, then immediately executing a maneuver known as an Immelman. My mouth literally dropped open because an Immelman on takeoff in a Wildcat is a pretty unusual maneuver with very little room for error. As I was watching this unfold, a friend walked up to me who had actually been a WWII FM Wildcat test pilot. He made a big deal out of Joe doing the maneuver at the Airshow and that worried me even more.

After the show I didn't want to make a scene about it, knowing that a father has to be pretty careful when dealing with a son on such weighty matters as independence and judgment. You don't want to seem over protective and at the same time you don't want to let something go that you think is dangerous either. So when Joe and I went to Fond du Lac to open for their Airshow, I turned the occasion into an opportunity to bring up the subject; it would be our first serious disagreement over flying.

"Joe," I said, as we were getting ready to climb into our airplanes and taxi out for takeoff, "I think this runway is a little short. I can't see an Immelman on takeoff." Joe just smiled while nodding his head then climbed into the Wildcat. We taxied out in front of the crowd and roared in formation down the 4000 foot runway. No sooner did Joe come off the ground and flew to the end of the runway, he rolled right up into an Immelman. I was furious despite the fact that it was a beautifully executed and very well controlled maneuver. Immediately upon landing I was venting my pent up anxiety and anger to Joe. After some heated discussion he agreed that he would increase his minimum runway length and the speed at which he entered the maneuver. I felt better after that but I still suspect that he had such a good feel for the airplane that the only reason he agreed was to make me happy.

The longer Joe flew the Wildcat the better his aerobatic routines became. Before long his Airshow act was very well known around the country. One Airshow in particular was very unique; he performed it in St. Louis in front of the Arch and between two bridges that were only separated by 3800 feet. The promoters wanted a Warbird act that could perform an entire routine, from the ground elevation up, in that very tight airspace. No one was willing to do the Airshow but Joe didn't see any problem with it. I was especially amazed considering that Federal Aviation Regulations required he not get any closer than 500 feet to either bridge, effectively reducing the horizontal distance available for the show to 2800 feet! The day of the Airshow arrived and though I have no idea how much he had practiced for it, he performed flawlessly within the allowable airspace. President George Bush was in the audience.

I met President Bush years later and mentioned the act. He did remember it. He was a navy pilot in WW II and flew with Wildcats as a hunter killer team finding and destroying German submarines.

Sometime after that we got Joe checked out in the P-40. I had him study the P-40 operations manual then gave him a briefing as he sat in the cockpit and I sat alongside on the wing. He started the engine, taxied out, and took off.

After about ten minutes of not seeing the P-40 I thought I'd contact him on the radio and see if he was beginning to feel comfortable in the high performance WWII fighter. "Joe," I said, "how are things going?" "Great," he replied with obvious enthusiasm in his voice, "I'm just coming out of a Cuban 8!" Oh well, at least it was a pretty day to go joyriding.

It wasn't long before Joe was doing very sophisticated aerobatics in the P-40 at air shows; one crowd pleaser was a loop with a snap roll on top. My proudest moment, however, was when he flew our P-40, which is painted in the Flying Tigers colors, at Oshkosh during the 50th anniversary of the American Volunteer Group, the Flying Tigers. R.T. Smith, one of the original Flying Tigers, mentioned to me after watching Joe's Airshow tribute, that he had never seen a P-40 flown as beautifully. It would be the last flight Joe ever made in the P-40. Shortly after that he was killed while returning from Texas in his aerobatic Astrocraft after having been competitively accepted as a member of the U.S. Aerobatic Team; but he had achieved his dream.

Well known aerobic pilot Kermit Weeks said, "There goes a good opportunity for the team to win the upcoming aerobatic world contest".

CHAPTER 42

Horse Trading,
The Modern Way

One of the most gratifying aspects of owning a multi-faceted aviation business is that we have some flexibility. However, everything we do compliments and supports everything else.

Over the years we have encountered customers who wanted to purchase one of our simulators but acquiring the necessary capital was a problem. For instance, one of our prospects was highly motivated to purchase a simulator, and we agreed to set up a financing program. One afternoon he called and said he was unable to come up with sufficient down payment but suggested he had a Piper aircraft that was easily worth the necessary amount. Negotiations began to determine the value of the airplane verses the required down payment for the simulator. It is, in short, a modern version of horse trading. From our perspective, it makes sense to take a good airplane in trade. We get an opportunity to fly a different airplane, use it for business travel if appropriate, and then sell it later through our FBO to recover the cash for the down payment.

So it was one May Saturday that my son David flew myself and a friend to Gault Airport near Lake Geneva, Wisconsin to pick up the Piper Pacer. The airplane was sitting on the ramp when we arrived. Walking up to it I could easily see the similarity between it and the later Piper Tri-Pacer. The Pacer had conventional gear, meaning it had a tail wheel, while the more modern Tri-Pacer had a nosewheel. The Pacer had been built during the late 1940s and early '50s and this particular model featured a 135 horsepower engine.

The airplane was in fairly good shape, but since I had not flown one since 1953, I thought it wise to get a checkout from the mechanic who had been responsible for its maintenance. We went over its maintenance history, and he reacquainted me with the location of various switches and some operational pointers. Before long, my friend and I climbed in, taxied out, and took off. David took off at the same time in our Mooney and flew alongside us for a while to make sure that everything was okay. After a while he was convinced things were going well and let his much faster airplane slide away and pass us up. As we cruised along at 110 mph I began to think about the many aircraft we have taken in trade over the years so that schools could put a simulator into their flight training program.

The first airplane I ever took in trade was the aerobatic Great Lakes Trainer. It was a very popular airplane in its day. The airplane was widely used by aerobatic pilots because of its handling characteristics. It was modified to include a more powerful 200 horsepower Ranger engine similar to the one used in a PT-19. Over the years, I can recall acquiring from various schools a Cessna 310, two 1980 Cessna 152s, a Cessna 150, and a Piper Cherokee 140, and others, most of which ended up in our own flight school. The school from which we got the Cherokee, in a subsequent deal, traded in a 180 horsepower Bellanca Scout and a two-place Model 223 Schweizer glider.

I had the director of one western flight school call me and express an interest in our Frasca Model 141 flight simulators. We sent him literature and talked to him a number of times. One day he called and said he wanted to place an order for two 141s. I quoted him the price and he said, "You don't understand. I'm going to give you a Dehaviland Beaver in trade for one of them and pay for the second." I said, "I'll get right back to you" and hung up the telephone.

The Beaver is a highly respected, Canadian ex-military aircraft. Its unusual design and 450 horsepower engine make it one of the most sought-after aircraft for bush flying in rural areas all over the world. It has the reputation for being able to haul big loads out of unimproved, small landing strips. Being the aero nut that I am, my heart was pitter-pattering when I called him back. Using some effort to control my voice so as not to appear too eager, I said "Yes, it turns out that we can handle it."

My son Joe oversaw the installation of the two simulators and picked up the Beaver for the trip home. The following Sunday morning, as I pulled up to our airport after church, there it was sitting on the ramp. We enjoyed flying it for quite a while, putting it through its paces, and discovering why it is such a respected bush plane. And while we really enjoyed flying the Beaver (one can get really attached to some of these aircraft), the fact remains we take them in trade with the intention of selling them. The Beaver ended up in the hands of a Canadian customer who would put her to good use, and she left us with pleasant memories and some money to pay bills. Since then, its value has quadrupled.

CHAPTER 43

Tom Frasca And Aircraft Sales

I mentioned in another chapter that our son Tom enjoys buying and selling aircraft. It turns out he's actually gotten to be pretty good at it and has made quite a few very good deals.

Tom's first purchase was a Luscombe and he kept that aircraft for quite a while. He bought it at a time when both his brother John and I had our own Luscombes. For a while it seemed as if we were starting a Luscombe fan club. Tom had his tied down at Frasca Field until some high winds blew through and ripped it out of the tie downs. The airplane flipped over and was totaled. The insurance paid off on the hull loss. Tom bought the wreck and ended up selling some of the parts that survived. All-in-all, Tom came out pretty good on the whole affair.

Next came an aerobatic, stagger-wing type aircraft called a Hyperbipe; it was very enjoyable to fly. Later, it was traded in a deal that yielded a Cessna 310 twin, which we used at the FBO for quite a few years. Tom bought his own Cessna 310, originally used during the Korean War, and the engine gave up the ghost one day while he was flying it. He brought it back on one engine, just like a pro. Tom ended up selling the aircraft for parts, actually making a profit on the deal.

Yet another, very nice, aircraft Tom bought was a Navion Rangemaster. It was built after WW-II by the same company that manufactured the P-51 Mustang. Based on the North American Navion, it had a sliding canopy. Sometime later, the Ryan Navion was built by another manufacturer, and it featured five seats and a 260 hp engine. The Ryan version had a fairly good cruise speed, was capable of flying for extended periods, and was very comfortable.

Tom once purchased a rather unusual but exciting aircraft: a Howard DGA, originally built in 1943 for Naval service. The design was somewhat similar to that of the Beech Staggerwing, except for single engine and, with its 450 hp engine, could cruise at 170 mph. The Navy used it for transportation, instrument training, and whatever else came up in those days. This particular airplane had ended up after the war as an executive aircraft for the Shell Oil Company and was painted in their corporate colors. All things considered, it was somewhat of a macho airplane for civilian use.

Tom took possession of the aircraft and set about learning to master its finer points. After he'd flown it for quite some time and practice takeoffs and landings extensively, he still could not consistently land the aircraft smoothly. Tom was unsure of what he was doing wrong and finally located someone who had flown the aircraft professionally. He called the pro and asked him what it takes to make consistently smooth landings. The pilot asked him, "how many landings does it take to get a good one?" "Only about one out of four is smooth," Tom lamented. The pro chuckled and said, "That's about the best you can expect!" Tom thanked him for his assistance and hung up the phone. Tom sold the airplane soon afterward as he was ready for another.

CHAPTER 44

Lake of the Woods
(an adventure without airplanes!)

In my early years at the University of Illinois one of my favorite places was a recreation area about 12 miles west of Champaign-Urbana. Lake of the Woods had a really nice landing strip situated between a man-made lake and a golf course. I had a 1946 Aeronca Champ in those days and I, and a number of my friends who owned their own airplanes, would fly there on sunny, warm days to relax and escape studying. In the days before I met Lucille, it was a favorite place of mine to bring a date and fly in for a picnic lunch.

One sunny afternoon many years later, I decided to leave work early and take two of my grandsons to Lake of the Woods. With the landing strip long gone, we drove. We parked the car, found some sturdy fallen branches to use as walking sticks, and set out on an adventure to explore the area. We arrived at an appealing clearing at just about the time my enthusiasm for exploring was beginning to diminish. The kids, of course, had yet to tap into their energy reserves and began to further explore the local area while I stretched out in the grass on a shady spot.

Combing every inch of the surrounding area, the kids began discovering golf balls. First one, then another, then several more until their collection began to grow rather dramatically. After the first two or three discoveries, however, the hypnotic swaying of two shade trees, strategically located on either side of my prone body, began to take their toll. I must have been deeply contemplating how nature, in her infinite wisdom and knowledge, had placed those two trees in just the right position to block the sun from striking anyone laying in precisely the spot where I was located. I had no idea that the kids had amassed enough golf balls to open their own driving range.

My profound contemplation about the position of the trees was rudely interrupted, after about 15 minutes, by the honking of a horn and someone yelling. I sat upright, looked around, and found a man yelling at me from a truck. It seems we had wandered onto a golf driving range, which certainly explained the apparently limitless number of golf balls the kids had been collecting. Sure enough, upon inspection, all the balls had little stripes around them! It was difficult to explain to the kids why they had to give their treasure trove to the man at the driving range but eventually they understood and did the right thing by returning them.

CHAPTER 45

Personal Values Age Like Fine Wine

The first weekend in June, 1995, was an Airshow at the former Chanute Air Force Base in Rantoul, IL. Since the closing of the base, I had been actively supporting a movement to turn the entire facility into an industrial air park. Conversion to civilian use was moving forward positively, if not quickly, and the Airshow was just one more planned event to garner public support.

The committee asked if I would be willing to participate in the Airshow by flying my P-40 and "shooting down" a Japanese Zero that would be "attacking" a B-25. I thought long and hard about it, because I was such a strong supporter of the project, but in the end chose not to do so.

I had only recently taken the P-40 out of the hanger, after a long winter's rest, and, quite honestly, didn't feel very comfortable with the idea of flying it in an Airshow. At first, the decision struck me as odd; I had never really hesitated to do something like that in the past. But upon reflection, it occurred to me that as one grows older some very subtle things begin to happen.

We all acknowledge that aging causes some decrease in timing, responsiveness, even memory, but what we often fail to realize is how much our values change with age. As our lives become more entangled with responsibilities, we begin to put personal whims on the back-burner and start considering what is the prudent and proper thing to do.

Lucille and I always enjoy getting together with the folks who fly the air shows and that weekend was no exception. Most of them spent a couple of evenings with us at Lucille's Flying School and Hot Dog Stand. And, of course, some of the Airshow pilots flew their aircraft over, so we ended up with our own, impromptu Airshow at Frasca Field.

A couple of pilots were from Canada and flew FAT Hornets; they were a real sight to see. It prompted me to pull out the P-40 and make a few low passes so everyone could get a good look at that beautiful airplane. As always, the P-40 just purred along beautifully. Later on, the Team America pilots showed up with their SF-260s. The 260 has a side-by-side cockpit and one of the pilots invited me along for a ride. We flew from Frasca Field over to Chanute and back; the airplane handled beautifully. That particular group of pilots had a terrific act and had won some very prestigious Airshow awards.

There must have been about 25 pilots flying the Chanute Airshow and most of them congregated at Lucille's Flying School and Hot Dog Stand on Saturday evening. They began talking about flying over Champaign on Sunday morning to drum up business for the Airshow. I got caught up in the conversation and said I'd fly the P-40 alongside them.

The next morning Lucille and I went to 8 AM mass, and then out to breakfast with a few friends. As we were about to go into the restaurant I looked up and saw the B-25 flying overhead; they had gotten a much earlier start than I had expected. I watched the B-25 with mixed emotions. On the one hand, I felt that I should be up there in the P-40, right off his wingtip. On the other hand, going to church and breakfast on Sunday mornings with Lucille and family friends is a very important part of my life. As I sat there eating my oatmeal and sourdough toast, I thought to myself "What's happening?"

To Lucille's great surprise, instead of going to the Airshow on

Sunday, I suggested we hop in the Mooney and fly up to Chicago Lakefront Airport for a stroll. We brought along our grandson Nic. As it happened, the Chicago Blues Festival was going on nearby and Nic, who at age 16 was a budding trombone player, was captivated. So, despite my not having flown in the Airshow, it was a very pleasant and enjoyable weekend.

Later, with the weekend only a memory, I recalled how on another occasion, I left an Airshow at Hamilton, Ontario, Canada on a Saturday because the next day was Father's Day. I simply felt I should be home for Father's Day. I found myself reflecting about personal values and realized that, as one ages, family begins to overshadow ambition and other interests. The more I thought about it, the more it appeared to me that, values, like fine wine, mellow with age.

CHAPTER 46

There Are No Old, Bold Pilots

There is a saying in aviation: There are old pilots and there are bold pilots, but there are no old, bold pilots. Over the years, I have tried to take that saying to heart by outlining a risk management program for myself. Unfortunately, that is sometimes easier said than done.

Some years ago I was flying home in my Wildcat from an Airshow in Kalamazoo, MI. After awhile in the air I could see that the weather was deteriorating and it quickly got bad enough that I decided I had better make a precautionary landing enroute. I found a nice, little airport quickly but it had a fairly short, grass runway. I circled the field once to take a look at the wind sock and determined that there shouldn't be any problem for the Wildcat, so I entered the pattern and landed.

As I taxied to the operations building I saw a small group of people standing there looking at me. It turned out they were thrilled by the arrival of an honest-to-goodness warbird and greeted me warmly. I explained my situation to the airport manager and he said there was room in their hangar but I would have to fold the wings to fit it inside. Well, that was great fun for everyone standing there watching me and I spent quite a bit of time talking about the aircraft.

Eventually, the crowd began to disperse and I was faced with the problem of getting home. The airport manager called a rental car agency that drove a car to the airport for me to use. We filled out the necessary paperwork and I got into the driver's seat. Before even attempting to start the engine I automatically reached down and pulled what I assumed would be the parking brake handle. I have gotten into that habit with my own car, not wanting to drive away with my parking brake locked up. Unfortunately, the rental was different than my car and the hood promptly popped up. Both the rental agent and I chuckled as he snapped the hood back down. I then started the car and without giving it a second thought pulled the hood release a second time, popping the hood open once again. I did this a total of four times before I finally got things under control. The rental agent was no longer smiling as he pushed the hood down for the fourth time. Fortunately, the drive home that afternoon and return to the airport to pick up the airplane the next day were uneventful.

I'm funny about that sort of thing. To this day I still keep checking to make sure the stem of my wrist watch is pushed all the way in; a habit acquired from having to wind a wrist watch. Oddly, it has been many years since I've owned a watch you have to wind but I keep checking it out of habit. Now that constant need to "check up" on things may seem a bit strange and in the case of the watch and rental car, perhaps it is, however, I don't let it bother me a bit.

Over the years I have lost quite a few friends and acquaintances. Of course there are the "normal" reasons such as World War II, Korea, and Vietnam. Some have committed suicide or even been murdered, although boating, automobiles, motorcycles and other similar types of accidents have taken a far greater toll. Somehow these things seem to be a tragic but a normal part of life.

The friends whose deaths have bothered me the most are the ones that have flown into mountains, crashed due to poor weather conditions, or just run out of oil or fuel. The ones who died because they exceeded the structural limitations of the aircraft or perhaps miscalculated while doing low-level aerobatics. It bothers me so much because more often than not they were preventable. Not that I haven't made my share of mistakes where little more than good fortune pulled me out of harm's way, but I do like to feel, in most cases, it's because I've been careful. Being careful, paying attention to detail, checking and checking again are really nothing more than a form of insurance policy. Today, we call it risk management.

It's funny, people don't think twice about buying insurance for their house, boat, car, aircraft, health and even life. The concept is simple enough: we buy insurance and if something goes wrong we get money that, we hope, will make up for the loss or at least help ease the pain and suffering. We even buy liability insurance to protect our assets in case we are sued. So why is it that so few pilots practice personal risk management? I don't mean the simple things like checking the weather or doing a preflight, though there certainly are pilots that don't even do those things. I'm referring to living their life, day-to-day, evaluating what they are doing and the potential harm that might come to them by doing it. Let me give you a simple example.

I like to take care of my cars and particularly dislike getting dents on the doors from parking to close too someone else's car. They open their door without regard for your car and suddenly you have a dent in your door. I make a conscious effort to find parking spots that are at the end of the parking lane or otherwise put my car in a position less likely to result in someone opening their car door into mine. When I have no choice but to park between two cars, I will try to find a space between two newer cars that don't have dents themselves. I have been quite successful over the years and my existing car shows no dents after five years of ownership. It is practicing situational awareness and the concept is the same whether you are flying an airplane or parking your car. Of course, sometimes it takes me longer to figure these things out than other times. I can clearly remember the days before I had this risk management mind set.

I happen to like to ride a bike for exercise and relaxation. I used to ride with no riding gloves, helmet, or substantial body protection that would help me in case of a fall. One day I was travelling downhill at a rather high rate of speed when a cat ran out in front of me. There was no time to avoid it so I ran into the cat and flipped over the handlebars onto the street. I guess past instincts from wrestling and having played football subconsciously took over as I broke the fall properly. It was just by chance that I happened to be wearing a jacket that day. I didn't get badly scraped and luckily I didn't hit my head. Ironically, the bike and I both sustained some damage, but the cat got up and ran away appearing unharmed.

The straw that broke the camel's back, and darn near my own, occurred after I got in the habit of riding my bike with no hands on the handlebars. Actually, it wasn't even that simple, the reason I wasn't holding onto the handle bars was because I was doing upper body exercises while riding. I was pretty successful at doing that for quite some time until one day I got a bit overzealous and threw myself out of balance. In trying to recover I managed to shift my weight in such a manner as to cause the front wheel to turn somewhat. The result was both dramatic and instantaneous; I fell off the bike at a fairly high rate of speed. Once again I was very lucky and didn't get seriously injured but this time the lesson wasn't lost. Shortly afterwards, I bought and began wearing a riding helmet and gloves, and also made a point to wear protective clothing. Today, I am very careful where and how I ride my bike and haven't had any problems since. That was my first conscious effort at developing a personal risk management program and it has carried over into my flying and all aspects of my life.

Another major area of concern is my health. I have lost friends as a result of their unhealthy lifestyles including: Over-eating, drinking, smoking, and generally not keeping physically fit. My experience has been that smoking catches up with you around age 60; I've had several friends retire only to die shortly afterwards due to a smoking-related disease. What a terrible loss for family and friends. No doubt about it, my pet peeve is smoking. I understand all things being equal, a non-smoker can count on an additional 17 years of life over their smoking counterpart. I will admit that passing 80 has not stopped me from an occasional martini before dinner or a little wine with my meals, but I do exercise regularly and my wife sees to it that we eat properly. Unfortunately, I love desserts, especially hot fudge sundaes, but as I grow older I hope to control even that a bit more. So what does all this have to do with flying?

I have a large and diverse collection of aircraft that ranges from a Piper J-3 Cub to a 2500 horsepower Spitfire and Turbo Commander and partnership on a jet. When you regularly fly so many different aircraft you have to take extra precautions. For me, that starts with being extra careful right from the beginning when we restore them to like-new flying status. All our aircraft are carefully and properly maintained. I am very fortunate in that we have excellent, well qualified mechanics working in top notch restoration and maintenance facilities. Of course, another important part of risk management is knowing your own limitations.

I am well aware, as I grow older, my hearing, eyesight, thought processes and reflexes are somewhat diminished. However, I work hard and plan ahead to reduce the chances that I get into a position that will compromise my physical limitations. For instance, our mechanics assure that every aircraft we fly is always in good operating condition and especially before each flight. We give them a thorough preflight check and make sure they have the proper type and amount of fuel and oil. Whenever possible, I start the fighters with someone standing by who holds, and is qualified with a fire bottle.

After completing the proper engine start, run-up and checks, I really make it a point to assure that the field conditions are appropriate and safe for the proposed flight. In particular, I like to use a grass runway for the fighters because you can run up and down them with the car to make sure everything is okay without bothering normal airport traffic. I also consider what is at both ends of the runway. At my own airport, we are almost surrounded by open fields which certainly gives me more options should I have a problem. For the same reason, I always try to take off with the canopy open in case something happens; it's much easier to get out of a problem airplane when the canopy is already open.

I have even been so safety conscious as to ask for a clear airport when flying one of the aircraft that are a bit new to me, If someone is giving flight instruction in the pattern, I ask that they hold a little way away from the airport and I tell them I am willing to pay for the time involved. The peace of mind knowing that I have a clear airport pattern available to me in the event of a problem, or just rusty flying skills in that airplane, is well worth compensating anyone for their inconvenience.

Another aspect of knowing your limitations deals with having too strong a desire to get somewhere by a certain time. Too often I have made the mistake of committing myself to going to an Airshow only to experience bad weather enroute making it very difficult to get there. I've lost too many friends who crashed flying to, or from, air shows during bad weather conditions. The same situation occurs when you're on your way home and really want to get there. There is a real tendency to let your emotion overrule your intelligence and the result is often disaster. So concerned am I about this issue that we have developed a flight training syllabus using our simulators that trains the pilot from the first lesson to deal with issues of weather. In fact, we teach student pilots to control the airplane first by reference to instruments before visual reference. The syllabus includes a total of three hours of instrument flying in our simulator and two hours in the aircraft before they are ever allowed to look out the window. Not only does this make the rest of their flying easier, when you learn instruments first, contact flying is a lot easier, but if the pilot does get caught in instrument conditions he knows how to safely make a 180 turn and fly out of it. At that point the pilot can reassess the situation and take appropriate action. It's not the way I, or most of my friends, learned to fly many years ago. In those days we hadn't heard the expression: "There are old pilots and there are bold pilots, but there are no old, bold pilots. Unfortunately, we had to learn that lesson the hard way.

A Brief History of
Frasca International:

Frasca International is located on Frasca Field, an FBO owned and operated by the Frasca family. The field also houses Frasca Air Museum which includes Rudy's collection of WWII aircraft. The facility, built in 1990 has over 85,000 square feet of office and manufacturing areas. A high bay manufacturing area allows for production of multiple Full Flight Simulators. The factory includes a machine and wood shop, standard production area, custom production area, offices and shipping and receiving areas.

Rudy Frasca serves as Founder and CEO and John Frasca serves as President of Frasca International. His siblings, Mary, Tom, Bob, Peggy, Liz and David are also involved in the business as are several in-laws and grandchildren. Many of the Frasca family and several employees are active pilots. Frasca International employs approximately 190 people in various departments. It is this fundamental love of aviation that drives the company to succeed in their mission to provide the tools to train safer pilots.

Products and Reputation

Over the years, Frasca simulators have developed a reputation for realism, reliability and affordability. As the number and reputation of Frasca simulators in use grew, the name "Frasca" began to be used as a generic term for simulators, becoming in effect a household word in the aviation training community. Rudy's company continues to work hard to maintain the good reputation that Frasca simulators have earned. Although the company has grown dramatically, Rudy's original mission remains the same: to design and manufacture high quality and reasonably priced flight simulators for training pilots worldwide.

Frasca International is an innovator in many areas. Under Frasca's direction, the company led the industry in the development of cost-effective simulation for single and twin reciprocating engine, pure jet and turbo-propeller fixed wing simulation, and helicopter simulation. Frasca International has developed a significant custom simulator market.

Frasca takes pride in providing customers with highly authentic and reliable duplication of the performance and characteristics of actual aircraft. In addition, Frasca simulators have a well-deserved reputation for long life and easy maintenance. It is estimated that over 90 percent of the over 2,500 simulators built since the company's inception in 1958 are still in operation today.

Customers benefit from Frasca simulators in many ways. They are used as primary and advanced simulators to teach flying techniques and procedures, including emergency procedures.

Military organizations use the simulators in much the same manner, but go even further with their instruction. Military simulators are used for mission rehearsal, tactical exercises and cross-training. Because of the highly accurate replication of actual aircraft characteristics, the simulators substantially reduce the training hours pilots have to spend in the real aircraft – time that can be used for actual missions.

As of this writing, Frasca International has delivered over 2500 devices in some 70 countries worldwide. Products range from the new Mentor™ AATD to custom Full Flight Simulators. Frasca's standard product line includes the Mentor™ and TruFlite™ devices. These "off the shelf" devices can also be customized for each end user. Custom devices for all aircraft types are manufactured to FAA, JAA or equivalent qualification standards. Frasca has recently delivered devices for aircraft such as the Diamond, Cirrus, CRJ, King Air, Baron, Citation, Bonanza and others. Helicopter flight training devices have become an extremely important product line for Frasca. Over 90% of U.S. aviation colleges are currently using Frasca flight simulators.

With such a wide product range, Frasca is known worldwide as the "Comprehensive Source for Flight Simulation." In addition to the actual Flight Training Devices, Frasca manufactures its own visual system, TruVision™ Global, which is available with a wide range of visual display systems and their widely used Graphical Instructor Station (known as GISt™). www.frasca.com